SPIRITUAL DECLUTTERING

40 DAYS TO SPIRITUAL TRANSFORMATION AND PLANETARY HEALING

BRUCE EPPERLY

Energion Publications
Gonzalez, FL

ISBN10: 1-63199-643-6
ISBN13: 978-1-63199-643-6

Library of Congress Control Number: 2019932430

Energion Publications
P. O. Box 841
Gonzalez, FL 32560

energion.com
pubs@energion.com

TABLE OF CONTENTS

The Spirit of Simplicity 2

    'Tis A Gift To Be Simple 3
    It's About Time!...9
    From Spaced Out to Spaciousness 15
    So Others May Live 19

Forty Days of Spiritual Decluttering........................21

    Week One 23
        First Things First!
    Week Two 38
        Blessed To Be A Blesssing
    Week Three...51
        Prophetic Prayerfulness
    Week Four...66
        Finding Spiritual Perspective
    Week Five..80
        Call And Response
    Week Six...94
        Grace and Gratitude

Group Study Questions...103

    Session One 103
    Session Two 105
    Session Three...106
    Session Four 108
    Session Five 110
    Session Six 112
    Session Seven 114

THE SPIRIT OF SIMPLICITY

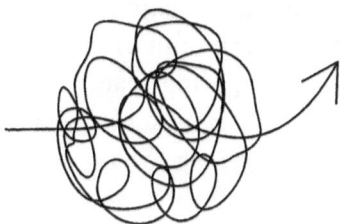

Chapter One

'Tis A Gift To Be Simple

Do you want a more abundant life? Do you want to live more fully and faithfully? Do you want to find a way to work hard and live well, to be committed to great causes and also have time for faith, family, and friends? Do you want to work to change your world, while experiencing calm amid the struggle? Do you want to live more simply and lessen the complexity of your life as part of your responsibility to the well-being of the planet and its peoples? How we answer these questions can be a matter of joy and sorrow, relationship and alienation, and life and death.

While decluttering our lives seems like a good idea, simplicity is far from simple for many of us. Caught in the complexities of clutter of mind, body, spirit, work, and environment, many of us need a pathway to spiritual decluttering. We need to simplify our lives as a way of discovering what is truly important. We need to get rid of the clutter so God's light can shine through. In the words of the poet William Wordsworth, many of us admit:

> The world is too much with us; late and soon,
> Getting and spending, we lay waste our powers;—
> Little we see in Nature that is ours;
> We have given our hearts away, a sordid boon!

We know that we need to simplify our lives, not just in terms of the clutter in our homes and offices, but the cumber that weighs down our spirits. We would like to experience greater joy, freedom and creativity. We want to let go of unnecessary obligations so we can experience greater focus, vitality, and love.

A good life involves the interplay of rest and activity and contemplation and action. Activity energizes and delights and brings new possibilities into the world. God gave each of us unique gifts and in embodying these gifts in the world, we bring beauty to the earth and add to the joy of creation. As the philosopher Alfred North Whitehead asserts, the process is the reality. We are meant to be active and push the limits of possibility. Without action, our minds, bodies, and spirits rust. We lose our growing edge. Our energy is depleted and our lives become uninteresting. Yet, we also know that too much activity and busyness can wear us down and distract us from what is truly important in life. A saying attributed to Carl Jung rightly addresses the dangers of a life solely devoted to action: busyness is not of the devil; busyness is the devil.

A good life also involves the interplay moments of reflection and rest. We need to refresh our spirits and rejuvenate our bodies. We need time apart to reclaim our spiritual GPS and gain perspective on our daily lives and civic involvements. Stillness and solitude nourish the spirit and give us perspective. Yet, rest without action, and contemplation without commitment, also depletes our energy, blunts our vision, and renders us so heavenly minded that we are no earthly good. Finding that right blend of action and contemplation is essential to a creative, meaningful, and socially responsible life.

A good life is characterized by the interplay of calm, vitality, and change. There are many paths to personal wholeness, and no path fits all persons nor all times of our lives. The balance between rest and activity is constantly shifting. The path we take forward depends on a lively integration of personal gifts, personality type, age, environment, vocation, and relationships.

The great religious traditions note the importance of contemplation in a life committed to action. An insightful reading of the gospel account of the relationship of two sisters, Mary and Martha, provides a vision for holistic living.

> *As Jesus and his disciples were on their way, he came to a*
> *village where a woman named Martha opened her home to him.*
> *She had a sister called Mary, who sat at the Lord's feet listening to*

what he said. But Martha was distracted by all the preparations that had to be made. She came to him and asked, "Lord, don't you care that my sister has left me to do the work by myself? Tell her to help me!"

"Martha, Martha," the Lord answered, "you are worried and upset about many things, but few things are needed—or indeed only one. Mary has chosen what is better, and it will not be taken away from her. (Luke 10:38-42)

At first glance, Martha gets the short end of the deal, relationally and biblically. Her efforts, so necessary to the dinner party, appear to be downplayed and criticized by Jesus. A deeper reading of this passage tells another story. Martha's work is valuable but Martha is busy, so busy that anxiety clouds her enjoyment of Jesus' presence. She is so distracted by her agenda and the tasks in front of her that she forgets to welcome her guest. Many of us can relate to the activist Martha. She wants things just right. She wants to be in control of the outcome. She wants give Jesus the respect he deserves as a reflection of her affection for him. Yet, she is so anxious to be the perfect hostess that she forgets the reason for her preparation – to be with Jesus, enjoy his company, and share in a good meal and lively conversation. The point of the story is found in Jesus' counsel to her, "you are worried and upset about many things, but few things are needed – only one." Martha is so distracted by the trees of preparation that she forgets the forest of hospitality. Martha needs to learn that spiritual simplicity, being present in this unique and holy moment, does not mean laziness or disengagement, but a sense of what is truly important over the long haul and in this fleeting moment of time.

As I imagine the story of Jesus' interaction these sisters, Jesus also has a few words for Mary. He delights in her relational attentiveness, but after a while he invites her to get to work. "Say, Mary, why don't you give your sister some time with me? Can you make sure the table's set and pour me another glass of wine? Maybe, you and Lazarus can clean up after dinner, so Martha and I can go on a walk in the starlight. After we get back, I'll help out, too!"

Jesus lived a dynamic and busy life, but Jesus was also present in the moment. He constantly balanced activity and rest, and then moved forward to the next encounter with focus, intentionality, and compassion. Even interruptions, and Jesus' life was full of unplanned meetings, didn't take Jesus off course. Mark's Gospel describes a day in the life of Jesus:

> As soon as they left the synagogue, they entered the house of Simon and Andrew, with James and John. Now Simon's mother-in-law was in bed with a fever, and they told him about her at once. He came and took her by the hand and lifted her up. Then the fever left her, and she began to serve them. That evening, at sunset, they brought to him all who were sick or possessed with demons. And the whole city was gathered around the door. And he cured many who were sick with various diseases, and cast out many demons; and he would not permit the demons to speak, because they knew him.
>
> In the morning, while it was still very dark, he got up and went out to a deserted place, and there he prayed. And Simon and his companions hunted for him. When they found him, they said to him, "Everyone is searching for you." He answered, "Let us go on to the neighboring towns, so that I may proclaim the message there also; for that is what I came out to do." And he went throughout Galilee, proclaiming the message in their synagogues and casting out demons. (Mark 1:29-39)

Jesus was busy, at least on the outside. He went non-stop from task to task, healing, teaching, and sharing a meal. As occupied as he was, there is no hint of anxiety, overwork, or compassion fatigue. He welcomed interruptions as opportunities for healing and hospitality. Perhaps, the key to Jesus' spiritual focus was his prayer life. At daybreak, he withdraws to a quiet place to commune with the Holy One. In that quiet place dedicated to communicating with God, he refocuses, finds direction for his life, and then lives out his vocation to preach good news throughout the countryside.

Jesus knew how to declutter. He knew how to put first things first and shape his life around his vocation and values. He had a mission, a clear vision of his vocation in healing the earth, and that mission guided his steps and framed his schedule. Active, though he was, Jesus lived out of the quiet center we see in holy women and men throughout the ages – in Gautama Buddha, Mother Teresa of Calcutta, and Mahatma Gandhi. They changed the world, but first of all, they changed themselves, moving from fragmentation to simplicity and distraction to focus. They were, in words popularized by Gandhi, first of all, the incarnation of what they wanted to see in the world in terms of their spiritual lives, decisions, and behaviors.

Our goal in the days ahead is to explore the dynamic process of spiritual decluttering by learning to live more simply in everyday life. Simplicity, as we will discover, is initially a spiritual issue, and then an issue of environment, consumption, and schedule. From inner simplicity comes a sense of calm that clears the clutter of our lives and enables us to have healthy environments and occupations. Spiritual simplicity enables us to discard the inessential and delight in the essential, whether at work or play. The spirit of simplicity, evident in Jesus' own lifestyle enables us to recalibrate our Spiritual GPS so that we might live abundantly and serve gratefully. Our spiritual simplicity, embodied in an uncluttered life, enables others to experience greater largesse and soothes our planet's distress.

In the next few chapters, we will reflect together on the fundamentals of spiritual decluttering as these relate to time, space, and survival. Our quest for a simple spirit-centered life challenges us to move from self-interest and individualistic consumption to world loyalty and compassionate care. Spiritual decluttering is a matter of daily practice, reflected in a forty day adventure. The number "forty" is not intended to be legalistic. It is a metaphor for an abundant journey, an adventure that brings wholeness to our lives, whether we walk with Hebrews and Jesus in the wilderness or go on a forty day voyage with Noah and his family. In that spirit, I invite you to take as many days as you need for the journey. In fact, spiritual decluttering is a lifelong adventure of decision-making and discovering what is truly important over the long haul and moment-by-moment.

Spiritual decluttering is not "one more thing to do," and get over with quickly; it is a way of life. We need soul food and not fast food to nourish our spirits. We need to add to the calm and centeredness of life, and not frenetically seek perfection even in our spiritual lives and relationships. In the walk of life, the "journey is home," as theologian Nelle Morton asserts. In that spirit, I want to thank the members of South Congregational Church, Centerville, Massachusetts, who sponsored a series on spiritual decluttering during Lent 2016 and in particular, Jan Fletcher, who coordinated the series and supported my focus on the spiritual dimensions of the decluttering movement. So let us begin our journey in song and prayer, knowing that we journey with the One in whom we live and move and have our being.

> 'Tis the gift to be simple, 'tis the gift to be free
> 'Tis the gift to come down where we ought to be,
> And when we find ourselves in the place just right,
> 'Twill be in the valley of love and delight.
> When true simplicity is gained,
> To bow and to bend we shan't be ashamed,
> To turn, turn will be our delight,
> Till by turning, turning we come 'round right.[1]

---

1   Elder Joseph Brackett, Shaker spiritual leader, "Simple Gifts."

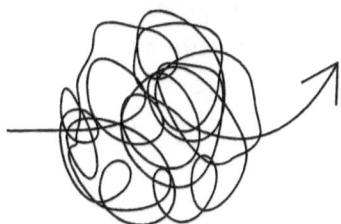

CHAPTER TWO

IT'S ABOUT TIME!

Our attitudes toward time can heal or harm us. According to physician Larry Dossey, many persons suffer from time, or hurry, sickness. They rush from one place to another, often without any clear sense of direction or priority. Like the white rabbit from *Alice in Wonderland,* they are constantly "late, late, for a very important date," even though they are often unsure of where they are going at any given time. Overscheduling has become a way of life for many of us. Stress has become a sign of commitment as professionals and parents vie with one another for the busiest, most booked, schedules. Those whose lives are characterized by calm are often judged as lacking commitment to their professional lives or the organizations they serve.

Our attitude toward time is both personal and cultural. It is related to our attitudes, scheduling, and expectations, many of which reflect our culture's values and not our own well-being. Do you remember the automobile commercial that elevated the USA over Europe because of the fact that we work longer hours and take shorter vacations? As I viewed the commercial, I wondered if focusing on long hours at the workplace as a sign of excellence truly adds meaning to our lives or quality to our work. Is having an expensive motor vehicle worth the sacrifice of time with family, recreation, and service to the community?

Our culture encourages busyness and touts the value of working hard and playing hard. It also promotes consumption, which often requires us to spend longer hours away from family and friends, as the pathway to happiness. Sadly, despite our proclamation of family values, family time is often sacrificed for professional and monetary interests. We neglect what we claim is most important – healthy relationships and time with friends and family – to maintain our personal and cultural consumerism. The shadow side of time sickness is the reality that many persons – including single parents, struggling to get by financially – are forced to work two and three jobs to provide adequate food, housing, and health care for their families.

We do have a choice. We can move from hurry sickness to spacious commitment. We can see time as our friend, abundant and joyful, and not our enemy, scarce and flowing away from us like sands in the hour glass. Living abundantly requires that we declutter our schedules as well as our homes. While many aspects of our schedule are out of our control, we can change our attitudes so that we can redefine what is urgent, necessary, and unnecessary and liberate ourselves from the tyranny of the temporal. We can clear the detritus of our lives so that landscapes of beauty may burst forth.

Decluttering is ultimately a spiritual issue, of priorities and spending the right balance of work, prayer, contemplation, re-creation, and rest. Abraham Heschel described the Sabbath as the sanctuary of life. On the seventh day, God rests. God resists the temptation to over-function and take control of everything. The divine rest or withdrawal, allows creaturely freedom and creativity to emerge. Although I believe that God is both omnipresent and omni-active, I also affirm that God is not omnipotent in the sense of determining every event in its entirety. Each moment incarnates God's loving vision, but God's loving vision is inspirational and guiding, not controlling. God prizes freedom and creativity at every level of life, and encourages our own creativity and freedom, congruent with the well-being of those around us. God makes space for rest in God's own schedule – God's providence balances freedom and creativity, so that we can not only act but also rest.

According the biblical tradition, the divine sabbath inspires the human sabbath. We are called to be fruitful and abundant in our lives, but our fruitfulness depends on rest as well as action. A number of years ago, we lived near an orthodox Jewish synagogue in Potomac, Maryland. Every Saturday morning, the Jewish Sabbath, scores of families, who located near the synagogue, could observed walking to the temple. While many of us might find their behavior legalistic, it reflected a number of spiritual values central to a healthy and fulfilled life: trust in God's care, when we aren't on duty; our dependence on others for our well-being; and the very real need for rest, relaxation, family life, prayer, and study. Set apart as holy from other days, the Sabbath reminds us of the holiness of every moment and our need to let go of control so that God's wisdom can guide our path.

Do you remember the Sundays of your childhood? If you're a certain age, like myself, you remember that the mood of Sunday differed from the other six days of the week. In small town Salinas Valley, California, where I spent my childhood, church was the center of our lives. The stores were closed, sports activities were suspended, restaurants remained shuttered till the noon church rush, and the screen of movie theatre, the "Reel Joy," was dark till the 3:00 p.m matinee. Since those slow-paced days of the Eisenhower era, life has radically changed. Some of us are on high alert for business 24/7, the demands of parenting keep us on the road from class to practice seven days a week, and stores vie our business with Sunday and holiday sales. The Black Friday sales have morphed into Thanksgiving bargains and Cyber Monday begins as we carve the turkey.

We can't go back in time, nor would many of us want to live in a world without the internet, Facebook, cable television, global travel, and advanced medical care, but all of these have cluttered our spiritual lives and filled our days to capacity.

The musical "Rent" asserts we have 525,600 minutes every year, and then asks "how do you measure a year?" Our lives can be filled to be brim with restless anxiety and constant clock checking or they can be "seasons of love." We can't change everything and we must chart our lives in relationship to the technologies of our workplace and domestic lives, but we can move from scarcity to spaciousness by spiritual decluttering.

In whatever way you understand Jesus relationship to human-kind, whether as Savior, model, healer, or companion, Jesus was busy. Although his days were full, often with unexpected interruptions, Jesus days were also spacious enough to embrace everyone he met in the Holy Here and Now of God's time. In the previous chapter, I described a "day in the life of Jesus" from the point of view of Mark's Gospel. (Mark 1:29-39). In that twenty-four hours Jesus did remarkable things that changed the lives of everyone he met. Jesus was no slacker! In the course of a day, he teaches, preaches, heals, and shares a working meal. Everywhere he goes throughout the day people demand his attention. Externally, he doesn't get a moment of rest. And, yet, he strides through the day with attentiveness, compassion, and care, responding to each moment as if it is the only one. Then, as a new day begins, he goes to a solitary place for contemplative prayer before setting out on the next day's holy adventure.

> *In the morning, while it was still very dark, he got up and went out to a deserted place, and there he prayed. And Simon and his companions hunted for him. When they found him, they said to him, "Everyone is searching for you." He answered, "Let us go on to the neighboring towns, so that I may proclaim the message there also; for that is what I came out to do." And he went throughout Galilee, proclaiming the message in their synagogues and casting out demons.* (Mark 1:35-39)

In quiet prayer, Jesus transforms time. He recovers the sense of time as "moving image of eternity," full and sufficient for every task. In stillness, Jesus finds his bearings, refreshes his mission, and sets his Spiritual GPS for the day ahead. In prayerful contemplation, Jesus connects with the Calm Spirit that undergirds the passage of time. He discovers that when he is aligned with God's vision for his life, he always has enough time to spare – to welcome, teach, heal, and challenge. Interruptions, and Jesus' journeys were often filled with interruptions, became healing opportunities and not nuisances. In the spirit of the musical, Jesus measured his days in love!

As we seek to rediscover the spaciousness of time we had as children and that mystics and lovers still experience, we would do well to follow the biblical admonition: "So teach us to count our days that we may gain a wise heart." (Psalm 90:12) "This is," as the Psalmist exclaims, "the day that God has made, let us rejoice and be glad in it." (Psalm 118:24) This moment is holy and is the gift of our 13.7 billion-year universe journey. We are soul stuff and star dust and need to remember that every moment is a potential epiphany and encounter with the One who always has enough time.

Time opens up when we ground it in God's spaciousness. When we let go of control, despite the importance of our personal visions, we discover that we have time enough for what is truly important. Time after time when I let go of my narrow ego-based agenda and follow God's guidance in the moment - helping someone in need, stopping a project to play with one of my grandchildren, putting down my laptop to engage a congregant, pausing to listen to someone share their heart – I discover I have all the time I need to flourish, to create, and to serve God and my neighbor. When I pause for meditation or contemplative prayer, I experience the intersection of this holy moment, the eternal, and the spaciousness of God's everlasting life in which time is spacious and filled with lifelines not deadlines!

In his inspirational book, *Tuesdays with Morrie,* harried sportswriter Mitch Albom, asks his favorite college professor, now dying of ALS, "What if you had one day perfectly healthy?" Morrie Schwartz then describes his perfect day: a breakfast of sweet rolls and tea, time with friends and family, a walk in a beautiful environment, then a dinner of duck or pasta, an evening of dancing, and then home to a wonderful sleep. At first Albom is disappointed at the apparent simplicity of the day. "After all these days, lying there unable to move a leg or foot – how could he find perfection in such an average day? Then I realized that was the whole point."[2]

---

2   Mitch Albom, *Tuesdays with Morrie* (New York: Doubleday, 1997), *175-176.*

That is the whole point! In time of your life, live – lovingly, simply, prayerfully, sacrificially, joyfully – one moment at a time in this wondrous flowing and lively, unrepeatable singularity, this Eternal Now where divinity and humanity dance and sing.

As a young boy, I played baseball nearly every summer day on an empty lot in our neighborhood. I was the youngest boy of my playmates and they often played good natured tricks on me. One summer afternoon, I hit a ground ball that barely made it past first base. As I stopped at the base, one of the boys purposely bobbled the ball, while another yelled, "You've still got time, Bruce." I got to second and he purposely overthrew the base, and once again one of the boys chanted, "You've still got time, Bruce." As I rounded third, the ball dribbled past me, and I streaked toward home with an inside-the-park homer. "I still had time."

That's become my motto as I look at time. "You still have time, Bruce." I am genetically predisposed to multi-tasking and enjoy having many projects on my desk. I am early for every appointment. But, I have discovered that I can be busy and calm and committed and at peace at the same time. I don't have to be stressed out to care. Nor do I have to hurry to be on time. As a matter of fact, when I am quietly connected to the well-springs of divine wisdom, I am more effective and responsive to unexpected crises the demands of those around me. When I regularly connect with God, I discover that I have all the time, talent, and treasure to flourish, love those around me, and respond to God's call. I always have the time I need in the season of love!

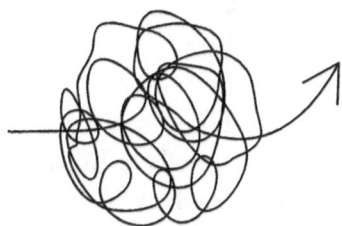

CHAPTER THREE

FROM SPACED OUT
TO SPACIOUSNESS

Virtually every nation and religious tradition affirms the existence of sacred spaces that reflect its community's deepest values. In the USA, citizens throng to the Lincoln and Vietnam memorials and Arlington National Cemetery, journey to the Grand Canyon, and take selfies at the Liberty Bell in Philadelphia. Muslims make pilgrimages to Mecca, Jews sojourn to Jerusalem, and Hindus bathe in the Ganges.

Celtic Christians, and the indigenous Druidic religion of Britain, describe these destination spots as thin places, where heaven and earth meet and where divinity becomes translucent to human beings. Native Americans experience divinity in rocks and streams and followers of Jesus travel to Bethlehem, the Jordan River, and Calvary's hill. God is present in every moment and every place, but certain places have been set apart as sanctuaries of the sacred, orienting our spiritual guidance systems in our quest to encounter God in time and space.

Cultures and faith traditions have sacred spaces, and so do we as individuals. Our holy spots can be our homes, neighborhoods, or distant places. Home is where the heart is, and our sacred spaces fill our hearts and replenish our spirits.

What is your sacred space? My local sacred space is Craigville Beach on the Nantucket Sound, where I walk nearly every morning, rain or shine, snow or wind. My sacred place at home is my study and prayer spot in the corner of my great room. This is the spot where I meditate each morning, read devotionals, study, and write sermons, blogs, and books. Virtually all of this text was written, sitting in my leather "arts and crafts" recliner, surrounded by books, note pads, and cups of coffee. When I asked the question, "Where is your sacred space?" at a spiritual decluttering seminar at our church, the participants noted personal sacred spaces such as "my garden," "my prayer room at home," "my computer table," "my art room," "my morning coffee in the sunroom," "my garden," and "our church's sanctuary." In another group, where I raised a similar question, I was greeted with responses such as "sailing on Nantucket Sound," "Gettysburg Battlefield," "Sedona," "my music room," and "a pond adjacent to our home." These sacred spaces center and calm us. They orient our lives and give direction to our daily activities. They are, T.S. Eliot avers, a "still point in the turning world...where past and future are gathered."

Recently, our congregation conducted a capital campaign to preserve and beautify our historic building. I reminded the participants that the fundraising was not just about brick, mortal, and woodwork, but the holiness of our historic spiritual home. Our church is, to many persons a sacred place, where couples repeated their wedding vows, children were baptized, learned about God and later married, and funerals and memorial services were held for parents, grandparents, and spouses. Within the walls of our church, we hear the stories of Jesus, discover the wideness of God's mercy, and receive comfort and direction in times of need. We treasure our sacred spots, because in their precincts we find meaning, healing, and spiritual orientation.

For many of us, our homes are more than wood, brick, and mortar or mortgage payments. "Be it ever so humble," our homes are places of rest, reflection, study, growth, and joy. Many of us experience a sense of calm, a version of the relaxation response, as we return home after a hard day's work, a medical appointment, or a holiday in a far-off land.

Yet, sadly many of our homes encumber our bodies and spirits with clutter than distracts and disorients. We suffer from the negative side effects of affluence. Too many things and too much clutter. Our consumption has made it difficult to navigate through our homes, and often long after clothes and furniture have worn out or gone out of style, we are still dealing with the burden of credit card debt.

In the spirit of Mitch Albom's question of Morrie Schwartz, imagine for a moment your ideal home environment in your current domicile. What images come to mind? How do you blend beauty and efficiency while living within your means? What is necessary and what is superfluous in terms of your home economics? In its "ordinariness," your home can be the perfect place for you and your family.

When Jacob woke up from his dream of a ladder of angels, traveling from earth to heaven and back again, he exclaimed "God was here in this place – and I did not know it. How awesome is this place, this is surely Beth-el, the house of God and gateway to heaven!" (Genesis 28:16-18, AP) Jacob embodies the spirit of William Blake's affirmation, "If the doors of perception were cleansed, everything would appear to man [humankind] as it is, Infinite!"

Could your home be the gateway to heaven and a sanctuary for divine creativity? Could you go to sleep, trusting God's care and the commitment of those who protect our streets and nation, and then awaken and say "how awesome to be in my home, however humble it may be, God is in this place and now I know it?" Is it possible that a closet or wardrobe in your home is the gateway to Narnia, and enchantment in the midst of domestic life?

The purpose of spiritual decluttering is to open the doors of perception and to help us see Infinity in our homes, workplaces, and environments. Spiritual decluttering allows us to see God's presence, often hidden by clutter and inconvenience. God is here, ready to be welcomed in our living rooms and bedrooms and inviting us to discard everything that hides the wonder of the glorious space and time where we stand.

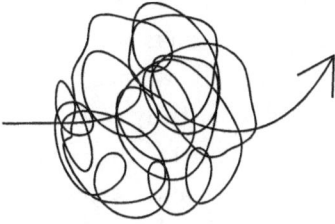

CHAPTER FOUR

SO OTHERS MAY LIVE

Decluttering is ultimately a spiritual and ethical issue, inviting us to reflect on our values and relationships to God and others. Do we live in a world, defined by scarcity or abundance? Do we place our own desires above others' well-being or do we live sacrificially, focusing on the welfare of the community as well as our own welfare? Are we isolated individuals, inspired by self-interest, or does our sense of connection inspire us to world loyalty?

St. Elizabeth Ann Seton, the first native-born American canonized by the Roman Catholic Church, once counseled, "Live simply, so others may simply live." Popularized by Mahatma Gandhi, this statement captures the heart of spiritual decluttering. It is truly a gift to be simple, to know what's important, and to conduct our lives in ways that heal our communities and the planet. Our habits of consumption have put the earth and its species at risk. Buying habits, and the incessant need to have the "latest and best" along with our idolatry of the Gross Domestic Product and shareholder profits have led to policies that privilege short-term profit over planetary survival. We have, as Pope Francis asserts, transformed our beautiful planet into a garbage dump by our overconsumption of the earth's resources. Our consumerist lifestyles have contributed to global climate change. Changing weather patterns have led to drought, extreme weather, famine, and have put millions of our brothers and sisters, not to mention our non-human companions, at risk. It is clear that the planet can no longer support the lavish lifestyles of even frugal North American and European consumers, who have gained the world but in the process are losing our souls and forfeiting our rootedness in our beloved Mother Earth.

Spiritual decluttering challenges us to self-awareness beginning with ourselves and our families and extending to embrace planetary well-being. We need to connect our plenty with others' scarcity and our purchasing with others' poverty. Conversely, we need to ask ourselves what is truly important to us and what truly constitutes abundant life. We need to consider what we can sacrifice so that others will experience the basic rudiments of life and beyond that the possibility of greater agency and well-being for themselves and their families. This is a matter of faith and ethics.

The biblical tradition challenges us to seek the realm of Shalom in which everyone has what they need, streets are filled with laughter, and communities see prosperity in terms of healthy relationships. Jesus promised, "Seek first the realm of God and you will have everything you need." (Matthew 6:33) The apostle Paul proclaimed that "God will supply our every need" (Philippians 4:19) and that "God is able to do more than we can ask or imagine." (Ephesians 3:20) These great promises remind us to put first things first: love of God, love of friends and family, love for the human community in its diversity, and love for this good and fragile earth. Connected with God, we have everything we need to flourish, give glory to our Creator, and serve our fellow creatures.

"So others may live" is at the heart of spiritual decluttering. It's not just about us; it's about the whole world. Simple living reduces stress, enhances our health, and transforms our understanding of time, moving us from scarcity to abundance. But, most importantly, when we honor the deep connections of life, our lifestyles honor God's creation and heal our communities.

As we declutter our homes, we may discover something more: we are decluttering our spirits, pruning away everything that gets in the way of God's light and our relationships with others. As the German mystic, Meister Eckhardt affirms, God is best known by subtraction. In letting go of spiritual and material clutter, we discover a treasure that exceeds our wildest imaginations – God in all things and all things in God. It is truly is a gift to be simple, and in true simplicity, we come round right!

Forty Days of Spiritual Decluttering

Over the next forty days, I invite you to embark on an adventure of spiritual simplicity. The Danish philosopher Soren Kierkegaard once stated that "purity of heart is to will one thing." Centuries before Kierkegaard, Jesus proclaimed "strive first for the kingdom of God and God's righteousness, and all these things will be given to you as well" (Matthew 6:33).

Author Frederick Buechner counsels, "listen to your life." Spiritual decluttering involves paying attention to what's going on with your heart, mind, and hands. Self-awareness, or mindfulness, involves observing both our thoughts and our actions. It involves noting when we are in synch with our highest values and when find ourselves at odds with our intention to live a more centered and faithful life. Simplicity of life is a matter of focus and intentionality. God's grace abounds, and we have everything we need to flourish. Yet, we need to open the door to grace by spiritual practices and concrete actions. Out of the listening comes action and the willingness, in the spirit of Quaker wisdom, to "let your life speak" in your environment, buying habits, stewardship, and generosity.

Each day's reflection involves the interplay of scripture, reflection, prayer, and action. A wise spiritual guide counseled, "pray as you can, not as you can't." In the course of the next several weeks, open to God's grace, doing the best you can to follow the daily reflections. But don't clutter your spirit with feelings of guilt or judgment. Don't worry about falling behind or forgetting to practice your spiritual exercises in the course of the day. Awaken to the grace of imperfection. Just the intent to live more simply already plants your feet on a holy adventure, filled with new energies and possibilities. As Jesus said, those who seek will find, and taking the first step on the path toward wholeness opens you to unexpected divine wisdom and energy. Live joyfully, live simply, love greatly, and rejoice in God's abundant life flowing through you to bring beauty and love to the world.

WEEK ONE

FIRST THINGS FIRST!

Spiritual decluttering begins with our vision of the world and ourselves. As we look at our place in the universe, we may be inspired to consider: Are we alone in the universe or do we live in a God-filled world in which guidance and inspiration can be found around every corner? Will God supply our deepest needs or do we live in a world of scarcity, heedless of our deepest spiritual desires? Accordingly, our spiritual adventure begins with an affirmation of the goodness of creation and our vocation as God's beloved children, created in God's image. As God's beloved, living in a God-filled world, we have everything we need to live abundantly while others live by scarcity. Just as we are, right now, in our wondrous imperfection, we are loved. Just as we are, we are enough. When we embrace the flow of grace, riches beyond belief – the riches of contentment, generosity, abundance, creativity and love – flow into our lives, making each day a holy adventure. Let each day this first week be a day of blessing in which you give thanks for the wonder of life and your own giftedness of God's beloved child.

Day One
"And It Was Good"

> *God saw everything that he had made, and indeed, it was very good. And there was evening and there was morning, the sixth day.* (Genesis 1:31)

Spiritual decluttering begins with affirming that the world around us is grounded in divine creativity and wisdom and that we are God's beloved children with all the resources we need to flourish in body, mind, spirit, and relationships. Augustine of

Hippo once asserted, "You have made us for yourself, God, and our hearts are restless until they find their rest in you." Much of our consumption is grounded in spiritual restlessness, the sense we are untethered from the world around us, with no resources to support us apart from our own efforts. When we recognize that, despite our imperfections, we live in a glorious, life-supporting world, we no longer need to fill the void with mindless consumption and frenetic action. Connected to God's creation and open to God's energy flowing in and through us, we have everything we need in terms of time, talent, and treasure. Living in the flow of divine abundance, we can give generously to those who lack our economic and social privilege, even if means sacrifices on our part. Sacrificial living becomes a joy rather than a burden.

Rabbinical teaching proclaims that the world was created good but not perfect. The perfect is complete and requires nothing. Our good, but imperfect, world provides countless opportunities for growth and adventure with each new day. Our incompleteness can be a gift, inspiring adventure, creativity, wonder, and vitality. Recognizing the goodness of life, we proclaim as each day begins, "This is the day that God has made, and I will rejoice and be glad in it." In living generously and gratefully, we claim our vocation as God's companions in healing the world.

Prayerful Decluttering. On this glorious day, bathe your senses in the beauty of the earth. Pause awhile simply to notice the beauty of the earth and the wonder of your own body-mind-spirit. Experience the world around you nurturing your body, mind, and spirit. Feel God moving through all creation and your own life. Recognizing that you are always connected with God and grounded in the graceful interdependence of creation, reflect on one action that you can do today to affirm the goodness and interdependence of life. You might go on a walk or find a park bench and just let your senses take in the wonder of life. You might consider what you really need to be happy and begin to think of ways to let go of what prevents you from experiencing the beauty life.

After a few minutes of silence, you may choose to pray: "Loving God, thank you for this good and beautiful world. Awaken me to wonder and give me a vision of what is truly important in life. Help me to prune all the unnecessary branches so that I might see your radiant light flowing in and through all creation. Amen."

A Simple Practice. Today, look around your home mindfully and prayerfully, noticing the essential, beautiful, and superfluous. What things clutter your home? What things around the house can you give away, or dispose of ecologically, to enhance your life? Devote five minutes today to prayerfully find a box or storage place – your "spiritual clutter box" - in which to place this clutter as the first step in letting go of it completely.

Day Two
"Belonging to the Universe"

And God said, "Let the earth bring forth living creatures of every kind: cattle and creeping things and wild animals of the earth of every kind." And it was so. God made the wild animals of the earth of every kind, and the cattle of every kind, and everything that creeps upon the ground of every kind. And God saw that it was good. Then God said, "Let us make humankind in our image, according to our likeness." (Genesis 1:24-26)

Are we lost in the cosmos, alone and without resources? Or, are we part of a wondrous and intricate dance of creation? Are we unique, totally different in kind from the non-human world? Or, do we live in an enchanted universe in which experience, value, and meaning are present in all creation? Is the universe mute and unfeeling? Or, do the heavens declare God's glory and all creatures praise God's grandeur?

The author of the first Genesis creation story (Genesis 1:1-2:4) describes our human uniqueness as part of the evolving and interdependent fabric of creation. We are not alone. God's wisdom is declared by the stars at night, the sun that greets us in the morning, and the mighty flow of rivers and the seas. God's creativity bursts forth in the sporting whale, the soaring eagle, and the sprinting gazelle.

Simplicity of life emerges from our recognition that we are connected and supported by all creation. Life in its abundance is everywhere and we discover our human vocations in light of our larger planetary environment. In the spirit of First American blessings, the Genesis creation story invites us to affirm, "with beauty all around us, we walk." We don't need to find meaning through consumption or ownership. The earth is God's and God is supplying every important need we have spirituality and relationally, if we but open our hearts, hands, and minds. Let God's glory, and the divine glory in you and your loved ones, satisfy your deepest needs and remind you that the best things in life are truly free and available each moment of the day. We don't have to purchase our way to happiness; it is ours for the sharing. We can proclaim, with Follett Pierpoint, "for the beauty of the earth, for the splendor of the skies, for the love which from our birth over and around us lies, God of all to you we raise this our hymn of grateful praise."

Prayerful Decluttering. In this practice, pray with your eyes open as you walk around your home and neighborhood, noticing the beauty of your environment.

And, then pray in a fashion similar to this: "Holy God, let me walk in beauty throughout today. I give thanks for the beauty around me (name the beauties you notice). May I add to the beauty of my home, neighborhood, and the planet by my every action. Amen."

A Simple Practice. Notice the beauty in your home and environment. Notice forms of clutter that detract from the beauty of your environment. Add something beautiful to your home and yard. Place an object that serves no purpose and detracts from beauty in your "spiritual clutter box" to give away, recycle, or trash.

Day Three
"We are Created in God's Image"

*So God created humankind in God's image,
in the image of God, God created them;
male and female God created them.* (Genesis 1:27)

The whole world is filled with God's glory, and so are you! The world begins in beauty and wholeness, not sin and brokenness. When we see a newborn baby, we are seeing the face of God, as Celtic wisdom giver Pelagius proclaimed. You are somebody. You are valuable. You are loved. When you look in the mirror, you see the image of divine wisdom and creativity. But, more than that, everyone reflects God's image. Reverence for life in all its human and non-human manifestations honors God's wisdom, love, and creativity.

Much of our heedless consumption and hoarding of possessions comes from the need to fill our inner emptiness. We may feel that we are not enough and so we fill our lives with frenetic activity and unnecessary consumption. We seek to dominate others to justify our own self-worth. Politicians bully and bloviate to make up for their feelings of inadequacy and inferiority. But, if the center is empty, nothing will ever fill the void. Only a relationship with our Loving Creator and God's beautiful creation can satisfy our longings. Discovering your identity as God's beloved, reflecting divine wisdom and love, and called to a glorious vocation as God's companion in healing the earth, is the greatest antidote to consumerism and clutter. Just as we are, our lives are abundant, and though we have a long way to go in terms of spiritual growth, God is with us and in us every step of the way, and even when we feel lost, the inner light of God still shines.

In discovering the divine image as our deepest reality, we no longer need to satisfy our spiritual hungers with possessions and actions that do not satisfy our yearning hearts. Right now, God's glory shines in our lives and lights our path toward wholeness and creativity. You are enough, you are beloved, you are God's own.

Right now, God is supplying our needs with more than we can ask or imagine.

Prayerful Decluttering. After a time of silence, look in the mirror and repeat, "I am created in God's image. I am God's beloved child. I have everything I need to flourish and serve God." Take a moment to write down this affirmation and repeat it throughout the day to deepen your connection to God.

Take a moment for prayer: "Creative Wisdom, I thank you for your image within me and welcome your abundant life. Help me to see your image in everyone and bring forth that image in myself and everyone I meet. Amen."

A Simple Practice. As a spiritual practice, take some time for prayerful contemplation, simply listening to God's voice with each breath you take. Then, ponder ways that you fill the "void" by consumerism, boasting, criticizing others, or eating or drinking in excess. Place these unhelpful paths to self-esteem in God's hands and ask God to fill you with the confidence that comes from knowing that you are God's child. Look at your schedule, noting activities that nurture the image of God within you and activities that detract from God's image. Discard any activities that no longer serve your growing identity as God's beloved child. Continue to place unnecessary clutter in your "spiritual clutter box." For intangible items, you can create a virtual "spiritual clutter box" in which to draw pictures or write down what you choose to discard.

Day Four
Holy Time

> *And on the seventh day God finished the work that God had done, and God rested on the seventh day from all the work that God had done. So God blessed the seventh day and hallowed it, because on it God rested from all the work that God had done in creation.* (Genesis 2:2-3)

A good life involves the interplay of action and contemplation. Times of rest and recreation are essential to our health and well-being. Built into the nature of reality is Sabbath time, even for God. According to Jewish mysticism, God's Sabbath rest, God's withdrawal from activity, makes room for creaturely freedom and creativity. Taking a Sabbath, even for a few hours each week, is a profound act of trust that life can go on in positive ways without our involvement. In letting go of control, and trusting God with the big issues of life, we experience a deep rest that radiates through every area of our lives.

In a world of constant addition, especially in terms of consumption, scheduling, and information, Sabbath operates by the principle of subtraction. In 2010, then Google CEO Eric Schmidt asserted that "every two days now we create as much information as we did from the dawn of civilization up until 2003." Schmidt presented a note of caution, "I *spend most of my time assuming the world is not ready for the technology revolution that will be happening to them soon.*"[3] In an era of ever-expanding information, Sabbath gives us permission to pause, notice, and open to the beauty of the earth and the joy of human relationships. Sabbath gives us perspective on our schedules and priorities and inspires wisdom to interpret the ever-cascading stream information characteristic of twenty-first century life.

Sabbath time provides the opportunity for profound spiritual decluttering. In dedicating a several-hour period to reflection each week, we learn to subtract items from our schedule. We put away

---

3   https://techcrunch.com/2010/08/04/schmidt-data/

the cell phone, turn off the computer, take a break from Facebook, and live in the Holy Here and Now. Some families choose internet Sabbaths from Saturday afternoon to Sunday evening. Others choose to go hiking rather than watch cable news or play on video games. Some choose to walk rather than drive or read devotional literature or novels rather than work-related or news feed materials. In spiritual subtraction, we say "no" to incessant information gathering and constant availability so that we can say "yes" to prayer and meditation, unhurried play and conversation with friends and family, and spiritual refreshment which comes from bathing our senses in the beauty of nature or inspiring our imagination with a good book. We say "yes" to graceful interdependence, trusting that God who cares for the lilies of the field and birds of the air will also take care of us. In times of Sabbath, we recalibrate our spiritual GPS and return to our daily responsibilities with a greater sense of priorities and a broader, less anxious, perspective. In practicing Sabbath, time becomes spacious rather than hurried and we discover we have all the time we need to flourish, care for our loved ones, and serve God.

Prayerful Decluttering. Intentionally commit a block of several hours or a whole day each week to simply "doing nothing," that is, to resting in God's grace in ways that refresh and reorient your life. Reflect during these hours of rest on what is truly important in your schedule and what is purely optional and can be discarded.

In a moment of prayer, ask God for wisdom to find a dynamic balance or interplay of action and rest, professionalism and prayer: "Holy One, let me trust the present and future to your care. Help me to let go of the inessential and optional and awaken to what truly brings abundant life for my loved ones, community, and myself. Amen."

A Simple Practice. Declutter your spirit and reframe your experience of time by looking at your week's schedule and then subtracting activities that are superfluous and have little impact on yourself and others. Focus prayerfully on what's truly important in life, and let go of the rest, placing these unnecessary activities in a virtual "spiritual clutter" box. Remember that what others deem urgent need not determine what is important to you.

Day Five
From Dominance to Relationship

Then the LORD GOD SAID, "It is not good that the man should be alone; I will make him a helper as his partner." So out of the ground the Lord God formed every animal of the field and every bird of the air, and brought them to the man to see what he would call them; and whatever the man called every living creature, that was its name. The man gave names to all cattle, and to the birds of the air, and to every animal of the field; but for the man there was not found a helper as his partner. So the Lord God caused a deep sleep to fall upon the man, and he slept; then he took one of his ribs and closed up its place with flesh. And the rib that the Lord God had taken from the man he made into a woman and brought her to the man. Then the man said,
"This at last is bone of my bones
and flesh of my flesh;
this one shall be called Woman,
for out of Man this one was taken."
Therefore a man leaves his father and his mother and clings to his wife, and they become one flesh. And the couple were both naked, and were not ashamed. (Genesis 2:18-25)

The story of the first couple is about relationship, and not biology or physiology. In the myth of the garden, first humans are given a task, to name the creatures of the earth. In the ancient world, names were meaningful and expressed a creature's relationship to God and her or his community. Naming implies knowing and empathy, and awareness and is based on relationships of interdependence and partnership. The first humans need companionship to survive spiritually, emotionally, and physically.

Although the non-human world is not adequate as the only companions for the first humans, non-humans have value, and can be objects of affection and care. Over thousands of years, humanity and the non-human world have entered into bonds of friendship, as is evidenced by our relationship with companion animals such as dogs and cats. These relationships to our non-human companions' empathy, emotions, and congruence with our own values.

Humans are intended to live in harmony with the non-human world and one another. The first couple are one flesh, one bone, and naked and unashamed. The description "it's complicated" does not, at this point, apply to our relationships with one another. Male and female, symbolic of humankind in its wondrous diversity, meet one another as partners, transparent to one another, with the vocation of nurturing and rejoicing in the good earth. While we cannot go back in time to the enchanted and mythical reality of that first couple, we can commit ourselves to simplifying and healing our relationships. We can recognize that relationships need Sabbath-time – time for recreation, relaxation, leisure, intimacy, and enjoyment. This involves letting go our attachment to technology, work, and information for a few minutes or hours a day, and rejoicing in the Holy Here and Now with our loved ones.

Healthy and loving relationships require time and space, and this means simplicity of attention, whether you are having dinner with your life partner, going to a movie with a friend, listening to a stranger's story, companioning a child, or caring for an elder. We can declutter our minds, hearts, hands, and schedule to do one thing at a time. As Ram Dass asserted, "be here, now." We can experience God's love flowing in our lives by being present to the task at hand and being attentive to the ones you love.

Prayerful Decluttering. When you come home, initially put your phone and calendar, apart from emergencies, out of sight. Studies indicate that even the presence of a cell phone on a table or desk detracts from intimacy and attentiveness. Spend the first few minutes – or longer - back home after work opening your heart to the ones who greet you, whether a child, grandchild, friend, life partner, or companion animal. Let go of any agenda. Give them your full attention. Listen and respond. Let your common identity as God's beloved – and this includes non-human companions – join you in moments of grace time. If you must work after hours at home, covenant with your companions for a set apart time, rather than multi-tasking and giving only partial attention to those around you.

Let this be your prayer: "Loving companion, open my eyes to your presence in the faces of those around me. Let me awaken to their divinity and by my love bring out the holiness in their lives. Amen."

A Simple Practice. Look at your schedule for the week ahead and set aside times for playful and open-spirited moments with loved ones. Look at what stands in the way of holy relationships and clear whatever relational clutter – on your end – that minimizes the quality of your relationships. Place these unnecessary activities in your virtual "spiritual clutter" box.

Day Six
Enter Complexity, and Hope for Simplicity

> *They [the first couple] heard the sound of the Lord God walking in the garden at the time of the evening breeze, and the man and his wife hid themselves from the presence of the Lord God among the trees of the garden. But the Lord God called to the man, and said to him, "Where are you?" He said, "I heard the sound of you in the garden, and I was afraid, because I was naked; and I hid myself." God said, "Who told you that you were naked? Have you eaten from the tree of which I commanded you not to eat?" The man said, "The woman whom you gave to be with me, she gave me fruit from the tree, and I ate." Then the Lord God said to the woman, "What is this that you have done?" The woman said, "The serpent tricked me, and I ate." (Genesis 3:8-14)*

What has been described as "the fall of humankind" is complicated, theologically and practically speaking. In looking at the myth of the "first" sin, certain questions emerge: Was it a fall downward toward the depths of degradation or a fall upward toward wisdom and creativity? Was it a loss of innocence or a gaining of maturity and possibility? In any event, the first humans found themselves unable to fully embrace the complexity of life and relationships. They became creators and yet their creativity leads to conflict, struggle, work, and alienation from the non-human world. Humanity embarked on adventurous exploration but lost a clear sense of its its spiritual GPS. While we can never go back to the age of innocence and enchantment, we can move forward to spiritual re-enchantment through immersing ourselves in prayer and meditation, and the rediscovery of beauty.

Growing up is challenging, as the first couple, and every growing child, discover. Moving from clutter to simplicity is also challenging, but it is the gift of intentionality and purpose. The simple life is the product of the healing of purpose – the integrity that comes from having a clear intention of your personal vocation and living out your vocation, your life vision, one act at a time. In my own decision-making, I have sought to follow the wisdom of Therese of Lisieux, to do ordinary things with great love; the practice of Saint Teresa of Calcutta to do something beautiful for God; and live out God's counsel to Abraham and Sarah, to bless everyone I encounter. When I follow these intentions, I realize that in the many activities of life, I am really only doing only one thing – blessing and beautifying this good earth and those around me. In following my vocation, I discover simplicity amid life's complexities and find guidance to discern the difference between the urgent and the optional, and the trivial and the important. When interrupted by others, I let these interruptions call me to prayerful loving service. In so doing, I find energy to support my loved ones and "miraculous" energy and creativity to finish what had been interrupted. Life becomes enchanted all over again!

Prayerful Decluttering. Simplicity of spirit emerges when we listen to the "still, small voice of God" through prayer and meditation. If you don't have a contemplative practice, you may choose to begin a form of "centering prayer" such as one of the following:

1) *Gently breathing in and out, with the intention of breathing in God's wisdom and energy and releasing stress and dis-ease.*

2) *A time of silence, beginning with the intention, "I am opening to God's guidance. Speak to me, Divine Wisdom."*

3) *Meditatively focus on a prayer word, such as "love," "peace," "God," "joy," "love."*

When your mind wanders, bring it back to your focus word and image, as a way of experiencing simplicity in a complicated world.

Let this be your prayer: "Let me be still, and know that you are my God, my companion, refuge, and support."

A Simple Practice. Prayerfully "ask, seek, and knock" in search of one daily practice that can help you move from complication to simplicity of life. What initially comes to you? As you receive guidance, take the first steps to embody the guidance you receive. Remember, your daily practice is a type of spiritual "PIN" number that you can always expand, refresh, or change.

Day Seven
Starting Over

Then the Lord God said, "See, the man has become like one of us, knowing good and evil; and now, he might reach out his hand and take also from the tree of life, and eat, and live forever"—therefore the Lord God sent him forth from the garden of Eden, to till the ground from which he was taken. God drove out the man; and at the east of the garden of Eden he placed the cherubim, and a sword flaming and turning to guard the way to the tree of life. Now the man knew his wife Eve, and she conceived and bore Cain, saying, "I have produced a man with the help of the Lord." (Genesis 3:22-4:1)

What happens when you are forced to leave the enchanted garden? What happens when life becomes work and work becomes difficult? What happens we are tranquilized by the trivial and anxious despite our affluence. Try as we wish, we can't go back to the garden. The child, who enters the world "trailing clouds of glory," becomes the anxious teen struggling with identity and the adult with too many obligations and too little time. We can't go back to the enchanted garden in its "dreaming innocence" but can we go forward to new enchantment, to an adult's sense of wonder and mystery.

The primordial couple are seldom given credit for their great achievement. We focus on their sin, but not their creativity and persistence. They begin again, and out of their creativity, culture is born in all its wonder and ambiguity. Despite their sin and alienation, they started over, giving birth to new paths in the human adventure.

In our own quest for spiritual decluttering, there will be plenty of starts and stops. As a wisdom teacher once stated, the spiritual life is a constant process of falling down and getting up again. Persistence and grace are essential to gaining a spirit of simplicity. To turn around right we must repent. We must turn around, let go of what no longer serves us, and take a new pathway, from death to life, and scarcity to abundance. This means eliminating the unnecessary and discarding what clutters our lives, despite our best intentions. It may mean pulling the plug on our addictions, not just the ones that are embarrassing or obviously destructive, but those addictions and compulsions that are socially acceptable and remunerative. We live in a society that worships success, workaholic behavior, greed, lust, competition, and consumption. We want to be better parents but our work styles marginalize our children. We speak about environmental destruction but rejoice in increases in unsustainable growth in the gross national product. We want to be healthy but fall into old eating and lifestyle habits. Yet, God's grace gives us the power and energy to begin again. Trust grace, let God love you, and begin again.

Prayerful Decluttering. In our quest for simplicity of life, we will find ourselves mired in complexity. We will clutter our minds, schedules, relationships, and homes. We will be tempted to fall into guilt and shame at our failures. While we need to recognize our mistakes and acknowledge our backsliding into old habits, we need to remember the grace that enables us to begin again and again and again and take the next step to wholeness. In your prayer life, follow the spiritual practice known as the Examen or examination of conscience. In this practice, look at your life without blinders, reflecting on experiences of success in your path toward spiritual decluttering. When have you followed the pathway of spiritual simplicity? When have you fallen off the path, and succumbed to old habits and addictions?

Ask for God's blessing and the opportunity to begin again with this prayer: "God, help me to see my life with fresh eyes, discerning what is important and what is not, and living gracefully through the day. Amen."

A Simple Practice. Prayerfully look at your "home economics," that is, your buying habits, expenses, and financial priorities. Our home economics reflect our spiritual priorities. Are your buying habits in line with your spiritual values? Where do you need to make economic adjustments to be more in synch with God's vision for your life?

Week Two

Blessed To Be A Blesssing

God tells the unexpected parents of the Hebrew people, Abraham and Sarah, that they are blessed to be a blessing. The graces of life are intended to flow through us to bless the world; first, our friends and family, and then our communities and the good earth. Our wealth is not our own, nor is it entirely the result of our intelligence or effort. When we spiritually flourish, our families and communities flourish. When our communities flourish, we and our neighbors flourish. The ethics of spiritual decluttering are grounded in the graceful interdependence of life. It takes a village to grow spiritually and our spiritual growth transforms the villages of which we are a part.

Day Eight
Leaving the Familiar

Now the Lord said to Abram, "Go from your country and your kindred and your father's house to the land that I will show you." (Genesis 12:1)

Spiritual decluttering can be like going from the familiar to the unknown. We have to let go of old habits and behaviors. We know the terrain of overbooked schedules, justifying our value by how busy we are, and unreflective consumption. It may not be pleasant, but it's what we know and there is great security in the familiar rush we feel at a busy schedule. We are uncertain and ambivalent as we imagine a future with time to spare, regular opportunities for prayer and meditation, and spiritual simplicity. We know ourselves by our frenetic calendars and adrenaline rush. We may not have much experience to saying "no" to other people's requests or choosing to spend time in meditation rather than watching television or going on the internet. Contemplative prayer may seem boring at first, or even frightening when we have nothing but God to fill our time.

I am sure that Abraham and Sarah wondered about the feasibility of leaving their home to go to a distant, and unknown, country. They had to radically change their lifestyle, give up their status in the community, and begin again as pilgrims and newcomers. They had to give up the familiar to embrace God's future. Yet, despite their misgivings they trusted that God would show them a pathway toward a better future for themselves and their descendants.

As we explore new values, behaviors, and lifestyles, we know that we, too, will have to give up certain familiar practices. But, we can sojourn into wilderness of possibilities knowing that God will guide us to new horizons of personal well-being and spiritual growth.

Prayerful Decluttering. After a time of silence, consider where God is leading you in the pathway of simplicity. What might it mean for you to "travel light?" To sojourn toward God's horizon of wholeness, what habits and behaviors will you have to give up? What are your hopes for the new land toward which you are going?

In a moment of prayer, ask God: "Loving Companion, show me the way through the wilderness. Help me let go of past behaviors and values that no longer serve me and those around me and open me to new possibilities for spiritual and relational growth. Amen."

A Simple Practice. Prayerfully look at your possessions as if you are going on a long journey: what one "important" item can you give up to gain greater peace of mind and travel more simply? Place it in your "spiritual clutter" box as a prelude to discarding it at some point in the future. Let this be a sign of your willingness to simplify your material life.

Day Nine
Blessed to be a Blessing

> *I will make of you a great nation, and I will bless you, and*
> *make your name great, so that you will be a blessing.* (Genesis
> 12:2)

Spiritual decluttering is about giving and receiving blessings. Some of us are too busy to bless. We are caught up in our agendas, late for important dates, and focused on our enjoyment, with little time to look beyond ourselves to respond to the needs of those around us. I find it humorous – and to some degree, sad - when I observe a family or a group of friends eating around table at a local restaurant, each of whom is involved in their digital devices, rather than addressing one another personally.

Blessing requires noticing and noticing occurs only when we take the time to pay attention to the world around us. Blessing comes from a spirit of abundance – abundant time, abundant energy, and abundant resource. But, mostly abundant time and attention. One of my personal affirmations is "I bless everyone I meet." To do this I have to remind myself to slow my pace in order to stop and notice. I have to look in the faces of others to see the face of God shining from them. I have to intuit our common humanity and their current emotional and spiritual condition.

Simplicity of spirit leads to a life of blessing. When I let go of my strangle hold on my agenda, I have the time to bless others and receive blessings in return. For those who bless others, there is always abundant life, regardless of their economic situations or the demands of their daily lives.

Prayerful Decluttering. Today, we focus on blessing persons around us. Begin with the affirmation, "I bless everyone I meet." Then, as you go about your day, pay attention to those around you. "Stop, look, and listen." You will discover that in the many details of your daily life, your vocation involves doing just one thing under many disguises, bringing beauty and well-being to the world by the blessings you give.

In the course of the day, also open yourself to noticing when you are blessed by a word or deed or an unexpected surprise.

Give thanks for the opportunity to bless and be blessed with this prayer: "Loving God, make me a blessing to everyone around me. Amen."

A Simple Practice. Focus on one person in your life who needs a blessing. Take time to pray for them and reach out with a call or note if this is appropriate. Look at your possessions: Is there one possession you might give away to bring a blessing to another person?

Day Ten
Praying One Place at a Time

> *Then the Lord appeared to Abram, and said, "To your off-spring I will give this land." So he built there an altar to the Lord, who had appeared to him. From there he moved on to the hill country on the east of Bethel, and pitched his tent, with Bethel on the west and Ai on the east; and there he built an altar to the Lord and invoked the name of the Lord. And Abram journeyed on by stages toward the Negeb.* (Genesis 12:7-9)

Wherever they stopped, Abraham and Sarah built an altar. At first, I suspect that they built stone altars to invoke God's presence. Later, I believe, their altars were affirmations that wherever they went, God was with them. The god of their homeland was now the god of their new land. Never alone, and always with divine resources at their disposal, they could live courageously in the wilderness through which they were traveling.

Each one of us is a pilgrim. We are on a journey even if we don't leave our familiar neighborhood. Each moment brings something new. There is never a moment like this Holy Here and Now. Each encounter can bring joy or sorrow, success or failure. We need to ground our journey in a sense of God's presence.

The Celtic Christians instituted a practice of "encircling." Whenever they embarked on a journey, they encircled themselves as they rotated in a slow circle, with their index finger pointed outward. This practice of encircling, accompanied by a prayer of guidance or protection, reminded them that they were always in the circle of God's protection.

We can build altars of God's presence or circles of care to remind us that God travels with us. God is the intimate companion who rejoices in our joy and suffers in our sadness. The encircling God is our companion, guide, and protector, who makes a way when we see no way forward. Let us build altars of prayer in every encounter, simply by invoking God's intimate presence each step of the way. These prayer altars remind us that wherever we go, we are home with God as our companion.

Prayerful Decluttering. Life comes at us fast, and we need circles of care and protection to remind us that we have the resources to respond to any changes in our environment or in our plans. As you go from one activity to another, draw a circle of guidance and care around yourself as a reminder that God is with you and that your only calling, whether you are at work or play, is to bless everyone you meet.

Let this be your prayer: "Circle me with love, circle me with protection, circle me with guidance. Amen."

A Simple Practice. Draw a circle in your imagination or physically around your residence. Ask God to protect your dwelling place and fill it with love. As you circle your house, think of one action you can take to make your home more beautiful to live in and your life less cumbersome in terms of your daily routines.

Day Eleven
Climbing with the Angels

> *Jacob left Beer-sheba and went toward Haran. He came to a certain place and stayed there for the night, because the sun had set. Taking one of the stones of the place, he put it under his head and lay down in that place. And he dreamed that there was a ladder set up on the earth, the top of it reaching to heaven; and the angels of God were ascending and descending on it. And the Lord stood beside him and said, "I am the Lord, the God of Abraham your father and the God of Isaac; the land on which you lie I will give to you and to your offspring; and your offspring shall be like the dust of the earth, and you shall spread abroad to the west and to the east and to the north and to the south; and all the families of the earth shall be blessed in you and in your offspring. Know that I am with you and will keep you wherever you go, and will bring you back to this land; for I will not leave you until I have done what I have promised you." Then Jacob woke from his sleep and said, "Surely the Lord is in this place—and I did not know it!" And he was afraid, and said, "How awesome is this place! This is none other than the house of God, and this is the gate of heaven."* (Genesis 28:10-17)

With nothing but a stone for a pillow, Jacob has an amazing dream. He dreams of ladder of angels, ascending from earth to heaven, and receives a glorious blessing from the Holy One. He awakens with fear and trembling, and stammers, "God was in this place – and I did not know it!" He renames the site of his dream Beth-El, the house of God.

What is surprising about this story is that the angels ascend from earth to heaven. The earth is chockfull of heaven, and the place where stand is the house of God. Celtic Christians spoke of "thin places," where the boundary between heaven and earth is erased, and early realities become a portal into divinity. Could it be that every square inch of earth is the house of God and that we don't need to go to heaven to experience God's presence?

Simplicity of life occurs when we open our eyes to God's presence and discover that we have everything we need right where we are. Meaning, insight, inspiration, and healing are present in this very moment. We don't need to fill our lives with possessions to be happy. We don't need to be busy to experience self-worth. God is giving me a blessing in the here and now that will guide us in our relationships, economic lives, and purchases. Then, we can exclaim, "God was in this place – and now I know it!"

Prayerful Decluttering. Once again, pray with your eyes open. Look around your home and your environment. Train your eyes for a "ladder of angels." Is your home the house of God? Do you find holiness here? Perhaps, you can clear part of your home from clutter and create a sacred space for study and prayer.

Let your prayer be: "God of dreams and revelations, let me experience your beauty in the place where I live. Let me experience spirits of healing and illumination to guide my life. Amen."

A Simple Practice. After discerning a place for prayer in your home, eliminate any cumber and clutter that might distract you from your goal of experiencing your environment as the house of God.

Day Twelve
Wrestling with God

Jacob was left alone; and a man wrestled with him until daybreak. When the man saw that he did not prevail against Jacob, he struck him on the hip socket; and Jacob's hip was put out of joint as he wrestled with him. Then he said, "Let me go, for the day is breaking." But Jacob said, "I will not let you go, unless you bless me." So he said to him, "What is your name?" And he said, "Jacob." Then the man said, "You shall no longer be called Jacob, but Israel, for you have striven with God and with humans, and have prevailed." Then Jacob asked him, "Please tell me your name." But he said, "Why is it that you ask my name?" And there he blessed him. So Jacob called the place Peniel, saying, "For I have seen God face to face, and yet my life is preserved." The sun rose upon him as he passed Peniel, limping because of his hip. Therefore to this day the Israelites do not eat the thigh muscle that is on the hip socket, because God struck Jacob on the hip socket at the thigh muscle. (Genesis 32:22-32)

Your quest for spiritual decluttering may involve wrestling with your understanding of God and your own desires. While the goal of the spiritual journey is alignment with God, the path may be filled with conflict. We may have to discard attachments that stand in the way of spiritual wholeness. We may have question our values and adjust our schedules. We may have to say "no" to certain actions that we have said "yes" to for years. We may have to let go of images of God which diminish our sense of agency and partnership in healing the world, along with shame-producing understandings of God. We may have to embark on journeys toward healing that require great effort, and a good deal of resistance on our part. The good news in our wrestling is that God is with us and makes a way when we perceive no way forward.

Jacob wrestled with God and received a blessing. When we clear away the physical and spiritual clutter of our lives, the light of God shines more brightly in our eyes, and we can bless the world.

Prayerful Decluttering. Take time throughout the day to find divine guidance with the following question: What issues do I need to wrestle with to experience greater integrity and simplicity in my life? Listen for the guidance you receive.

Let this be your prayer: "Wrestling God, let me find guidance as I wrestle with you in the quest for wholeness and simplicity. Amen."

A Simple Practice. Wrestling leads to acting. What one step can you take today in response to the insights you are receiving. The process may be painful and you may feel like you're walking with a limp for a while. But, sooner or later, you "will run and not be weary and walk and not faint." (Isaiah 40:31)

Day Thirteen
Be a Dreamer

Then Joseph said to Pharaoh, "Pharaoh's dreams are one and the same; God has revealed to Pharaoh what he is about to do. The seven good cows are seven years, and the seven good ears are seven years; the dreams are one. The seven lean and ugly cows that came up after them are seven years, as are the seven empty ears blighted by the east wind. They are seven years of famine. It is as I told Pharaoh; God has shown to Pharaoh what he is about to do. There will come seven years of great plenty throughout all the land of Egypt. After them there will arise seven years of famine, and all the plenty will be forgotten in the land of Egypt; the famine will consume the land. The plenty will no longer be known in the land because of the famine that will follow, for it will be very grievous. And the doubling of Pharaoh's dream means that the thing is fixed by God, and God will shortly bring it about... Let them [Pharaoh's overseers] gather all the food of these good years that are coming, and lay up grain under the authority of Pharaoh for food in the cities, and let them keep it. That food shall be a reserve for the land against the seven years of famine that are to befall the land of Egypt, so that the land may not perish through the famine." (Genesis 41;25-36)

We live in a throwaway society in which thrift is no longer a virtue. We are told on a daily basis that the key to happiness is found in consumption and that having more things will give us greater joy. As a society, we spend money we don't have, often racking up thousands of dollars in credit card debt. While purchasing goods does help the gross domestic product and increases employment in some fields, our consumption also contributes to the destruction of the environment and global climate change, especially since the cost to the environment is seldom factored on the balance sheets. Moreover, millions of North Americans live from paycheck to paycheck and cannot sustain an unexpected medical, household or automobile expense. Further, few of us have stockpiled non-perishable items in preparation for a long-term power outage or national emergency. While there are a variety of reasons for our inability to increase our personal savings, much of it is related to spending our money on superfluous items and a philosophy of instant gratification rather than patient saving that allows us to be generous to family members and persons in need.

Now, there is nothing wrong with using our resources for dinners out, dancing, movies, times with friends, learning opportunities, travel, and the creation of a safe and attractive environment. They can bring joy and growth to our lives and a good life involves times of celebration. Without abandoning creature comforts or being legalistic about our expenditures, we need to reflect on the spirituality of stewardship. We need to explore the relationship between our spiritual values and everyday expenses. What do our financial practices say about us in terms of what is truly important? Do we support our church and other benevolences adequately, given our income? Are we generous toward persons in need? Do we live an ecological economic lifestyle? What brings us true happiness on a daily and long-term basis?

Prayerful Decluttering. Prayerfully examine your spending habits. Where do you spend your money? Does your current lifestyle bring joy or anxiety? Are you "drowning in credit card debt?" Do you give generously to causes that are important to you? Are you able to save money "for a rainy day" or for retirement?

Let your prayer be: "Holy One, let me understand the true value of money. Let me discover true abundance. May my financial decisions bring joy to me, my loved ones, and the world around me. Amen."

A Simple Practice. After examining your spending habits, consider one area you where you might economize. Make a commitment to place half of the "saved" money in a savings account and the other half in a program that supports persons in need.

Day Fourteen
What do You Say to a Burning Bush?

> *Moses was keeping the flock of his father-in-law Jethro, the priest of Midian; he led his flock beyond the wilderness, and came to Horeb, the mountain of God. There the angel of the Lord appeared to him in a flame of fire out of a bush; he looked, and the bush was blazing, yet it was not consumed. Then Moses said, "I must turn aside and look at this great sight, and see why the bush is not burned up." When the Lord saw that he had turned aside to see, God called to him out of the bush, "Moses, Moses!" And he said, "Here I am." Then he said, "Come no closer! Remove the sandals from your feet, for the place on which you are standing is holy ground." He said further, "I am the God of your father, the God of Abraham, the God of Isaac, and the God of Jacob." And Moses hid his face, for he was afraid to look at God.* (Exodus 3:1-6)

Sometimes a typographical error can reveal an unexpected truth. As he was preparing his Sunday sermon some forty years ago, my mentoring-pastor George Tolman typed "what do you do with a burning *busy?*" instead of his intended word, "bush." He realized that one of the reasons we see so few burning bushes is that we so busy we have no time to pause and notice. Tolman's insight complements the wisdom of a rabbinical conversation in which one day a group of rabbis were arguing about why the bush Moses encountered was burning but not burned up. They went around and around with possible explanations until one of the group suggested, "the bush was burning but not consumed so that one day as Moses walked by he would notice it!" Day after day, according to this explanation, Moses walked by, lost in his own world and fretting about the tasks of the day, never noticing the wonder he passed by, until one day he paused to pay attention to God's message right in front of him.

I believe that God is omnipresent, that is, present everywhere and in all things. Practically speaking, this means that the providential guidance of God is hidden in every encounter and situation. When we pause long enough to notice, the humdrum world becomes a world of wonders in which divine messages come to us every moment of the day. We have choices each moment to attend to the burning bush or the burning busy. Take this morning: I am trying to finish a rough draft of the "forty days of spiritual decluttering" by Ash Wednesday to use as a Lenten devotional at church. At sunrise, I am typing away, working on today's lesson, when I hear footsteps coming down the stairs, and my five year old grandson who spent the night with us races to my chair with the intent on cuddling on my lap. I put aside my computer and he falls asleep on my chest. When he wakes up, he jumps off my lap and begins to draw pictures on his art table in the kitchen. I resume my writing, hoping for thirty minutes of focus. But, ten minutes later, knowing that I have been writing, he comes up to me again with the request, "Gabby (his name for "grandpa"), let's write a book together." Down goes the computer and up comes a little boy, intent of sharing his own creativity. While sometimes I simply need to finish a document in a timely fashion, I realize that nurturing this young child was at the heart of "spiritual decluttering." Childhood is fleeting, and the time I spend loving and shaping this young child is more important in God's eyes than a few pages of writing! Somehow when I let go of my schedule for a greater good, new energies and creativity emerge that make the task I put aside to respond to another's need go more quickly and successfully.

For those who take a moment to pause and notice, there are burning bushes everywhere. Look around! Move from multi-tasking to focusing on the holy here and now. God comes to us every moment, and when we pay attention, our lives will be joyful and whole.

Prayerful Decluttering. Today, ponder the relationship between the "burning bushes" and "burning busies" in your life. What adds zest to your life? What adds busyness without a blessing for your or others?

Make a commitment to slow down and see God's revelations strewn along your daily path as you pray: "God open my senses to your wisdom and insight. Help me see the burning bushes on my path and celebrate the beauty of this good earth. Amen."

A Simple Practice. Throughout the day, pause, look around, and notice. Let yourself be surprised and amazed by God's wondrous world.

WEEK THREE

PROPHETIC PRAYERFULNESS

What kind of world do you want to live in? What changes are you willing to make personally and corporately to live in the world that you imagine for yourself, loved ones, and children's children? A significant portion of scripture is dedicated to the prophetic writings. The prophet's focus on fairness, justice, and simplicity of life as central to faithful living is found throughout the First (Old) and Second (New)Testaments.

The prophets felt compelled to speak for God in challenging social situations. As they experienced what Abraham Joshua Heschel described as the divine pathos, God's sensitivity to the pain of the poor, dispossessed, and marginalized, they called the rich, famous, and politically powerful to radical spiritual and economic transformation. These words echo in our own times, where the gap between the rich and poor continues to increase. The prophets, as Walter Brueggemann asserts, proclaimed an alternative vision to the injustice that was rampant in the land. For the prophets, personal, economic, and political ethics could not be separated. Spirituality pertains to the whole of life. Faithfulness to God involves our pocketbook as well as our prayer life, our nation's budget as well as our personal stewardship. Our national life needs decluttering so that justice will "roll down like waters and righteousness like an everflowing stream." (Amos 5:24) In the week ahead, we will reflect on alternative visions, new possibilities, for our personal and political involvement, and discover our calling to live more simply so others can simply live.

Day Fifteen
Visualizing Peace

The wolf shall live with the lamb, the leopard shall lie down with the kid,
the calf and the lion and the fatling together, a little child shall lead them. (Isaiah 11:6)

Recently, I chuckled as I read a bumper sticker that counseled, "Visualize whirled peas." Though it was a takeoff on the quest for peace in our world, the humorous quote reminds us that we need to imagine a different world than the one we currently live in and then do what we can to make a peace a reality in our homes, city streets, and on the world stage. A glance at this morning's news tells us we have a long way to go. Whether we describe ourselves as liberal, conservative, or independent, we are regularly troubled by world leaders threatening nuclear war with words reminiscent of playground bullies, violence committed against Muslim citizens and immigrants, terrorist threats, school shootings, and gang-related murders. We know that our world can be different. We dream of a world in which former enemies become reconciled and children can play safely on city streets. We cannot be content with life as it is, but must claim Isaiah's vision of Shalom, written during a time of national turmoil, nearly 2,800 years ago.

Wisdom can be found in the words of bumper stickers. The peace we seek in our hearts and in the world will not come unless we transform our lives and institutions. One bumper sticker proclaims, "be the change you want to see in the world." One writer notes that this is a short summary of the words popularized by Mahatma Gandhi: "If we could change ourselves, the tendencies in the world would also change. As a man changes his own nature, so does the attitude of the world change towards him. ... We need not wait to see what others do."[4]

---

4   Brian Morton, "Falser Words were Never Spoken," *New York Times*, August 29, 2011. (http://www.nytimes.com/2011/08/30/opinion/falser-words-were-never-spoken.html)

In other words, we must not wait for the world to become a place of peace. We must become peaceful ourselves. We must guard our words and thought so that these promote justice and peace rather than alienation and violence, whether in our households, on Facebook, or in the political area. If we want peace, we must be peaceful, and live our lives with awareness that life can be different and that our own lives can contribute to transforming our communities and the world. Yes, go ahead and "visualize whirled peas" or "world peace," and then take the first steps in bringing a just and holy peace to every situation and relationship. Focus on bringing peace to every encounter. In pruning away anger and alienation, we will bring peace to our communities and experience the peace that passes all understanding, the peace of doing God's work in the world.

Prayerful Decluttering. Inner and outer peace are connected. In the course of the day, observe your reactions to various situations. Take your spiritual and emotional pulse throughout the day. When do you feel contentment? When do you feel anxious? When do you feel intimate with others? When do you feel alienated from others? What situations bring greater peace and greater anxiety? Visualize ways you can minimize feelings of anxiety and alienation. Feelings of peace do not lead apathy, but creative problem solving and peacemaking.

Let this be your prayer: Begin by taking some slow calm breathes, visualizing God's peace entering your body, mind, and spirit, followed by words such as, "God, I seek your peace. Let my every breath be a prayer. Let me inhale your healing love and exhale peace into the world. Amen."

A Simple Practice. In the course of your day, observe moments of peace and anxiety. Which of these moments of peace and anxiety are related to your decisions and values, both personal and economic? Which are related to information you receive from the news and other sources? While we cannot and should not retreat from the world, we can challenge our media viewing habits and household priorities that add unnecessary to our lives. We can separate the essential from the optional in our schedules to live more simply and mindfully.

Day Sixteen
Your Prophetic Calling

> *The spirit of the Lord GOD is upon me,*
> *because the Lord has anointed me;*
> *he has sent me to bring good news to the oppressed*
> *to bind up the brokenhearted,*
> *to proclaim liberty to the captives,*
> *and release to the prisoners;*
> *to proclaim the year of the Lord's favor.*   (Isaiah 61:1-2a)

What is your personal vision statement? These words from Isaiah were the polestar of the prophet's ministry to the Judah's ruling elite, spoken some eight centuries before Jesus began his own public ministry with these same words. (Luke 4:18) Jesus articulated a complementary mission statement, recorded in John 10:10: "I came that they may have life, and have it abundantly." Having a vision, or mission statement, whether individually or institutionally, helps us prioritize the use of our time, talent, and treasure. It enables us to decide between the essential and inessential, the necessary and optional, the urgent and unimportant. Our life mission determines our recreation, benevolences, and household purchases along with what is essential in terms of clothing and furniture. A vision statement focuses and simplifies our lives, and helps us set our priorities.

Jesus' mission inspired his ministry of hospitality, healing, and companionship with marginalized and dispossessed persons. His vision of God's realm ultimately led him to sacrifice his well-being for the healing of creation.

Discovering your vocation requires taking time to notice your gifts, talents, values, life experiences, and environment. Once again, we need to pause, notice, and listen to our lives. According to Frederick Buechner: *"the kind of work God usually calls you [in terms of vocation] to is the kind of work (a) that you need most to do and (b) that the world most needs to have done. ... The place God calls you to is the place where your deep gladness and the world's deep hunger meet*"[5] Discovering our vocation helps us prune away the cumber to the light of God's guidance can shine through. So, in the spirit of Frederick Buechner "listen to your life" and then, following the counsel of Parker Palmer, "let your life speak."

Prayerful Decluttering. Today, if you are able, go for a walk, guided by the deceptively simple question, "God, show me my calling. What is the most important thing I need to be doing to be faithful to you and those around me?" Let the many voices of your life come to the surface, and then pray for one to come to the surface as your guiding vision. In doing this on a regular basis process over a several-year period, I have come to realize that my vision and calling involve "being a force for healing, love, and beauty in every situation." You might attempt to write a personal mission statement to guide your actions, purchasing, and relationships.

Let this be your prayer: "Guide me, God of the Far Horizon. Give me a vision and the strength and energy to fulfill it in my daily life. Amen."

A Simple Practice. As you discern your vision, it is important to know that you have both a vision or visions for the long haul and a vocation for each new moment. Every moment and each day God speaks to us, giving us guidance for our journey. Listening to your vision, what changes to you need to make to your schedule and immediate environment to experience greater simplicity of spirit?

5   Frederick Buechner, *Wishful Thinking: A Seekers ABC* (San Francisco: Harper One, 1993), p. 118-119.

Day Seventeen
Encountering the Living God

In the year that King Uzziah died, I saw the LORD sitting on a throne, high and lofty; and the hem of his robe filled the temple. Seraphs were in attendance above him; each had six wings: with two they covered their faces, and with two they covered their feet, and with two they flew. And one called to another and said:

"Holy, holy, holy is the LORD of hosts;
the whole earth is full of his glory."

The pivots on the thresholds shook at the voices of those who called, and the house filled with smoke. And I said: "Woe is me! I am lost, for I am a man of unclean lips, and I live among a people of unclean lips; yet my eyes have seen the King, the LORD of hosts!"

Then one of the seraphs flew to me, holding a live coal that had been taken from the altar with a pair of tongs. The seraph touched my mouth with it and said: "Now that this has touched your lips, your guilt has departed and your sin is blotted out." Then I heard the voice of the LORD saying, "Whom shall I send, and who will go for us?" And I said, "Here am I; send me!" (Isaiah 6:1-8)

Sometimes our calling comes to us unexpectedly and dramatically. As I reflect on the story of Isaiah's encounter with God, I visualize a member of the nation's elite and educated class going into the temple for a few moments of peace in a time of time of national turmoil. Like most of us who attend church, Isaiah didn't expect to encounter the Living God in all God's grandeur during a worship service. But, out of nowhere, God shows up and everything is turned upside down. Isaiah realizes his imperfection and unimportance in relationship to the God of the Universe and stammers "Woe is me! I am lost!" only to receive forgiveness, a new beginning, and a question that will forever change his life. "Whom shall I send, and who will go for us?" God queries. Overwhelmed by the Divine energy of grace, Isaiah responds, "Here am I; send me."

I believe that God's voice calls to us every moment of the day. God's call comes to us through dreams, hunches, intuitions, encounters, reading material, prayer, and worship. God whispers in the maelstrom of conflicting voices that characterize daily life. When we listen, in all our fallibility, self-interest, and busyness, to God's voice, our lives gain orientation and focus. We can discern the highest possibilities for any given moment. We receive guidance for our decision-making and prioritization. Because God is constantly calling to us and all creation, our prayers to hear God's call are always answered, in accordance with our openness and willingness to follow the visions we receive. While we cannot claim to fully know God's will, we find guidance, direction, and energy – and a way is made when there appears to be no way – when we respond to God's call, "Here I am, send me."

Prayerful Decluttering. Throughout the day, pause to ask, "God show me the way." If you discern divine whispers, quietly respond, "Here I am, send me" and then respond in a way that is appropriate to your gifts and context.

Throughout the day, take time to pray: "Speak to me, Loving God, and help me listen and respond. Amen."

A Simple Practice. According to the prophetic writings, God is concerned with both home economics and national economics. Prayerfully look at your household expenditures, asking God to speak to you in terms of your domestic expenditures. Listen for divine wisdom coming to you as you reflect on expenses, home furnishings, entertainment, and benevolence. Where is God's wisdom guiding you? Take a first step to a more faithful, and ecologically sustainable, domestic economy. Where is God sending you to care for those around you?

Day Eighteen
The Justice Option

He has told you, O mortal, what is good;
and what does the LORD *require of you*
but to do justice, and to love kindness,
and to walk humbly with your God? (Micah 6:8)

What does God want from us? We have many gifts, talents, and possibilities. But, our vocation is not just about us; it is about the well-being of others. God wants us to fulfill our dreams, and God also wants us to support the dreams of others. Personal one-to-one healthy relationships are essential to our well-being and the well-being of others. More than that, we need to create communities of justice and compassion. We need to move from polarization and alienation to kindness and appreciation. We need to let go of selfish individualism and commit ourselves to expanding our sense of well-being to include our neighbors and strangers.

Take a moment to meditate once again on God's vision for us as a community and individuals: "what does the Lord require of you but to do justice, and to love kindness, and to walk humbly with your God?" How we achieve God's vision is a matter of resource and context, but the vision is non-negotiable and should be at the heart of every decision we make. We need to reflect on what it means for us to be humble in our relationships. What does it mean for you to practice kindness in a time of political polarization and national division? What is the meaning of justice in a society whose decisions often favor the wealthy over the poor and the powerful over the dispossessed? In what ways can your life give witness to Gods' vision of Shalom and justice for all creation?

Prayerful Decluttering. Simplicity of life is grounded in humility and kindness, both of which require letting go of our sense of superiority and separation. We are one with all creation. No person is alien to us. Throughout the day, be mindful both of your language and self-talk. Do your words and thoughts promote peace and understanding? Do your behaviors bring healing to your immediate community? As I write these words, I am watching images of another school shooting spree and feel heart-broken at the pain and trauma these youth will carry with them from now on. God's call through Micah to us challenges us to repent of our individualistic attitudes toward personal freedom and gun ownership and balance our own rights with our responsibility for the well-being of the children and youth of our land. What do we need to give up as a society to bring just peace to our schools and city streets? What personal behaviors will promote peace in the neighborhood and nation?

Let this be your prayer: "Holy God, let there be peace on earth; let peace start with me; let this peace be in my heart, words, and actions. Let my voice ring out for justice and healing wherever I find myself. Amen."

A Simple Practice. Jesus once counseled let your "yes" be a "yes" and your "no" be a "no." Today, experiment with simplicity of speech. Avoid negative, demeaning, polarizing, and judgmental language. Commit yourself to speaking healing words wherever you are. Challenge injustice with firm but loving speech.

Day Nineteen
Authentic Spirituality

But let justice roll down like waters, and righteousness like an ever-flowing stream. (Amos 5:24)

Spiritual decluttering is a matter of justice-seeking. The connection of unbridled individual consumption and corporate greed is intimately connected with poverty, domestic unrest, family discord, violence in our neighborhoods and city streets, substance abuse, and environmental destruction. The prophet Amos challenges the rich and powerful of Israel's social and political order to embody their faith in acts of personal and political justice.

We are embedded in the politics and economics of our community. Our communities are weakened by poverty and neglect, and our own lives are threatened by pain and injustice of the social order. We are, as Martin Luther King asserts, part of an intricate fabric of relatedness, in which I cannot be with I am intended to be until you are what you intended to be. We are complicit in the evils we deplore, but we can minimize our complicity in economic injustice, racism, and sexism. We can use our economic and ethnic privilege and power to work for justice and equity in our world.

As a Cape Codder, I experience the transformative power of water every morning as I gaze at the waves rolling in and out on Craigville and Covell's beaches. God's quest for justice will not be denied; it is an ever-flowing stream and a constantly surging wave. Today, let us catch God's wave of justice and righteousness and propel ourselves forward toward communities of compassion and healing. Let us choose life for our environment and future generations by living more simply.

Prayerful Decluttering. Amos connects water with justice-seeking. Water refreshes, awakens, and cleanses. We need spiritual cleansing as well as decluttering. If you consider yourself a person of privilege, you may choose to do the following spiritual practice: As you shower, visualize God's waters flowing over you, awakening, cleansing, and refreshing you for the day ahead. On this day of new beginnings, where do you need to be cleansed in terms of your complicity with injustice? Where do you need to be awakened to the pain of poverty and exclusion? Where does your spirit need to be refreshed so that you might have the energy to make the changes you need to make locally and globally for the well-being of persons and the planet?

Let this be today's prayer: "Let your justice roll down like waters, carrying me toward your realm of Shalom. Let me ride the surf of justice seeking in companionship with your wondrous waves of grace. Amen."

A Simple Practice. Identify one issue of significant pain and suffering in your community or nation. While you may not have policy advice for your representatives, you may have values counsel for them in their political decision-making. For example, if you don't have a specific issue – although groups like Bread for the World can be helpful in terms of legislative guidance – you may register concerns about issues such as fairness in the treatment of immigrants and refugees, environmental policy, poverty in your community, or gun violence in schools. You do not need to passively watch the news. You can let the news call you to prayer and action.

Day Twenty
Prophetic Justice

> *Hear this, you that trample on the needy,*
> *and bring to ruin the poor of the land,*
> *saying, "When will the new moon be over*
> *so that we may sell grain;*
> *and the sabbath,*
> *so that we may offer wheat for sale?*
> *We will make the ephah small and the shekel great,*
> *and practice deceit with false balances,*
> *buying the poor for silver*
> *and the needy for a pair of sandals,*
> *and selling the sweepings of the wheat."*
> *The* LORD *has sworn by the pride of Jacob:*
> *Surely I will never forget any of their deeds.*
> *Shall not the land tremble on this account,*
> *and everyone mourn who lives in it,*
> *and all of it rise like the Nile,*
> *and be tossed about and sink again, like the Nile of Egypt?*
> (Amos 8:4-8)

These are hard words, aren't they? They must have stunned the elite of Jerusalem, when they first heard them. They couldn't imagine their behaviors leading to the pain of others. Still, the prophet challenges them to look at the consequences of their values on the poor and vulnerable. The prophets presented an alternative reality to the injustice perpetrated by the wealthy and powerful of Israel. They imagined a world of Shalom, in which good work was honored, children could laugh at play, vulnerable persons were supported, and the wealthy's hearts were filled with compassion leading to sacrificial actions on behalf of the poor.

Sometimes you have to hear the bad news, the impact of your actions, to embrace the new good news of healing and joy. Receiving a negative medical or dental report can be unsettling and inconvenient. You may have to change your lifestyle, eating habits, work schedule, and dental hygiene. But, the good news is better health, increased longevity, and greater delight in simple pleasures.

Amos' word to the business and political leaders is painful and demanding. The path of injustice that they have taken will leads to poverty and social disorder. It may even lead to national destruction. The prophet Amos unmasks the illusion of those in power in business and politics, whose excuse is "it's not personal, just business; we don't mean harm, but we only have so much money to go around." In contrast, Amos asserts that all of our decisions are personal. A pen stroke puts thousands out of work; apathy about common sense gun regulation leads to mass shootings in Las Vegas, Newtown, and Parkland. The prophets then and now challenge nations that let the cumber of wealth, consumption, and power politics stand in the way of justice and peace.

We prepare the way for the coming Savior by clearing away the cumber of our personal and corporate lives. Perhaps, and on this "perhaps" our future depends, if we change our ways and become rich in spirit, rather than possession and power, our nation will truly claim its vision of "liberty and justice for all" and God will "crown our good with brotherhood – and sisterhood – from sea to shining sea."

Spiritual Decluttering. Once again, pray with your eyes open, as you look at the images presented by the media today. It might be pictures of parents grieving in the wake of another school shooting, Syria refugees washed ashore on a Mediterranean beach, immigration officers arresting a non-violent undocumented worker who has been in our nation for decades, or demonstrators shouting words of hate toward persons of color. Pray to keep your heart open and to stay faithful to God's calling for justice and peace.

Let us pray, each of us in our own way: "God whose love embraces all creation, let me have a heart for the world. Let me hear the cries of the poor and respond with compassion. Show me how I in my role as a citizen can support your arc of justice and compassion in our world. Amen."

A Simple Practice. Amid the many demands on your time, prioritize one area of social healing. It might involve calling your representative or the White House regarding immigration or gun violence. It might mean joining a non-partisan hunger and political groups such as Bread for the World and Better Angels or a non-partisan gun safety group such as Grandmothers Against Gun Violence. It might mean forming a group at your church to respond to hunger, poverty, or violence. We are the ones we've been waiting for, as poet June Johnson says. We can't wait for our legislators to do something beautiful for God. God needs our hands and hearts to bring healing to the world in one to one relationships and as citizens. God doesn't demand that we do the impossible, but that we be God's healing companions right where we are.

Day Twenty-One
Hearing God's Words

*The time is surely coming, says the Lord God,
when I will send a famine on the land;
not a famine of bread, or a thirst for water,
but of hearing the words of the Lord.
They shall wander from sea to sea,
and from north to east;
they shall run to and fro, seeking the word of the Lord,
but they shall not find it.* (Amos 8:11-12)

The prophetic tradition is profoundly holistic and relational. For the prophets, there is no separation between the sacred and secular or spirituality and ethics. Nor is there is a separation between God and humankind. God is constantly providing us with spiritual, ethical, relational, and political guidance. God also experiences the world in its joy and sorrow. Abraham Joshua Heschel states that the primary inspiration for the prophets was their experience of "divine pathos," the reality that God hears the cries of all who suffer and feels the pain of all who are neglected.

Amos warns us that when we close our hearts to the poor and vulnerable, we are also closing our hearts to God. Amos speaks of a "famine" of hearing God's word as a result of our lack of empathy and compassion. This famine is, however, not the final word. When we turn our hearts to the forgotten, we are turning our hearts to God. When we open to the pain of the word and respond with acts of compassion and transformation, we are opening to God's compassion growing in our own lives. God comes to us in all things: the gentle breeze, the rolling surf, the singing bird, the laughing child, the traumatized teenager escaping a shooting at her high school, a hopeless parent unable to feed her child, and an immigrant being berated because of his nation of origin. We live in a God-filled world, and as we respond, we will receive blessings beyond belief. God will fill our hearts with a surplus of joy, hope, and love.

Prayerful Decluttering. Continue praying with your eyes open as you watch the news, read the local paper, or observe relationships in your neighborhood. Pray for our leaders from the President to our local officials that they might gain a heart of wisdom.

In the words of prophets, ask God: "God of all, give me a heart of flesh, and take away my heart of stone. Let the currents of your love flow in and through me. Amen."

A Simple Practice. Touched by divine compassion, and in line with your spiritual values, make a gift to a person in need. It can be a grocery debit card, a contribution to a church agency such as Church

World Service or World Vision. Pray your gift as you visualize those who will receive your blessing, remembering that we are all in it together, and ask God to give you the resources and generosity to use your largesse to bring joy to the world. There is no "other," in God's world where everyone is joined in God's circle of love. We can give thanks to those who are the objects of our generosity, knowing that in the giving we affirm our unity and are blessed beyond measure.

Week Four

Finding Spiritual Perspective

Jesus went to a mountain to share his spiritual vision. While many scholars assert that the Sermon on the Mount is a collection of Jesus' sayings and not a sustained talk, Jesus' words on the mount reflect his ethical, spiritual, and theological vision. Jesus is inviting us to turn from the values of the world to God's values. In the spirit of Jesus' image of the vine and branches, Jesus is challenging us to prune anything that prevents us from experiencing God's light flowing into our lives in all its life-transforming and world-changing power. This week, I invite you to live with Jesus' message. Let it convict and transform your life, enabling you to let go of the inessentials so that you can experience the fullness of God's grace.

Day Twenty-Two
Blessings Abound

Blessed are the poor in spirit, for theirs is the kingdom of heaven.
Blessed are those who mourn, for they will be comforted.
Blessed are the meek, for they will inherit the earth.
Blessed are those who hunger and thirst for righteousness, for they will be filled.
Blessed are the merciful, for they will receive mercy.
Blessed are the pure in heart, for they will see God.
Blessed are the peacemakers, for they will be called children of God.
Blessed are those who are persecuted for righteousness' sake, for theirs is the kingdom of heaven.
Blessed are you when people revile you and persecute you and utter all kinds of evil against you falsely on my account. Rejoice and be glad, for your reward is

great in heaven, for in the same way they persecuted
the prophets who were before you. (Matthew 5:3-
12)

The path of spiritual decluttering can turn our lives upside
down. If we read the Beatitudes of Jesus superficially, our first
response might be, "If this is what it means to be blessed, I don't
want any part of it!" Jesus asserts that we can feel God's presence
in the most unlikely circumstances: grief and persecution. Blessing
doesn't come through possession or power, but in humility, justice-seeking, peacemaking, and acts of mercy. The blessed know
that they can't go it alone. Their experiences tell them that they
need God and each other.

In the biblical tradition, the person most pitied is the self-
made individualist, requiring no one but her or himself for her or
his happiness or success. The rugged individualist lives by the fragile illusion of independence, that can be shattered at any moment
by a stroke, accident, diagnosis, or collapse of the stock market.
Jesus tells the story of a successful farmer, whose sense of value
is wrapped up in his financial success. He builds a great barn to
store his bountiful harvest only to die the night that construction
finishes.

The blessed build their house on the rock of graceful interdependence. When the storms come, their reliance on God will get
them through despite any pain or loss they may experience. Those
who depend on their own powers and wealth have built their house
on shifting sands. When life's storms come, they lack a sure foundation and are washed away.

When we turn from independence to interdependence, we experience the blessing of divine companionship both as individuals
and as communities. Fully relying on God's graceful companionship, we discover that life's changes will not destroy us but may
ennoble us and deepen our faith so that our wounds can become
windows to God's grace and our weakness can inspire us to help
other struggling pilgrims.

Prayerful Decluttering. The theologian Paul Tillich once referred to a person's faith as involving their "ultimate concern," that is, the reality around which we center their lives and give allegiance, and from which they expect ultimate fulfillment and security. Tillich believes that much of the time we focus on secondary realities – power, health, youth nation, money, popularity, respect in the community – as ultimate despite the fact that none of these can deliver what they promise in times of crisis and need. Only God can be our ultimate concern; only God can fulfill the deepest desires of our hearts and give us the courage to face death in all its forms. In this practice of spiritual decluttering, consider your own personal "ultimate concerns." In what way are these related to God? After all, you can love the Creator by prayerfully loving God's creatures. Do you ever give these false "ultimates" your primary loyalty? In what ways might you love the world rightly by placing God at the center of your life?

Today, let us pray: "Holy God, help me to know what is truly important; help me to trust your guidance; and depend on your grace. Guide me so that out of my own interdependence, I will bless others. Amen."

A Simple Practice. Today, look deeply at your life. Upon what realities and persons do you most depend? Who depends on you for their well-being? Take time to give thanks for the graceful interdependence of life and make a commitment to bless in healthy ways those who depend upon you. Reach out with wisdom and compassion to someone whose spiritual or emotional well-being depends on your care. Be the face of God for them.

Day Twenty-Three
Becoming Light

You are the light of the world. A city built on a hill cannot be hid. No one after lighting a lamp puts it under the bushel basket, but on the lampstand, and it gives light to all in the house. In the same way, let your light shine before others, so that they may see your good works and give glory to your Father in heaven. (Matthew 5:14-16)

Our spiritual growth is a matter of call and response, and grace and commitment. God's light shines in and through each of us. But, often we hide God's light – the image of God within us – by our own behaviors and values. We hide God's light from others by focusing on things rather than relationships, and consumption rather than compassion, and we hide God's light from ourselves by values that see our own lives in terms of external markers such as cultural images of beauty, prizing superficiality over substance, and seeing our value in terms of productivity and ownership instead of God's love for us and our own unique beauty. Such false understandings of ourselves are revealed in the question, "What's he or she worth?" as relating to one's financial assets and property instead of the inner light of divine presence within.

We all want to stand out, some more than others. But, Jesus says we already stand out. We are God's light, and when we let the light of God flow through our own unique gifts and experiences the world becomes transparent to divinity. We don't need to prove ourselves to anyone; we are already loved and are embraced eternally in God's care. Seeing the light emerges when we see ourselves and the world with new eyes. Being the light occurs when we peel off the superficial externals and let the radiance of God's love shine through us to heal and transform the world. What do you need to peel off so that God's radiance shines through? What do you need to discard to see God's light shining in others?

Prayerful Decluttering.   In this spiritual decluttering practice, pause to find a comfortable chair. Set aside fifteen minutes for stillness. Begin by simply breathing, gratefully inhaling God's blessings. As you exhale, let go of any burdens or stress. Then, after a few minutes, visualize divine light entering you with each breath. Experience the light filling you from head to toe. As you exhale, let your light go forth into the world to bring healing to those around you.

Throughout the day, stop and pray: "Let your light shine in and through me, O God, to give light to the world and healing to those around me. Amen."

A Spiritual Practice. Today, make a commitment to do only one thing in your many different activities. Commit yourself to bringing God's healing and uniting light to every situation. Visualize for a second, the impact of God's light flowing through you in every situation and encounter. See this light in those around you and treat them – as well as yourself – as God's light bearers.

Day Twenty-Four
Letting Go of Anger

You have heard that it was said to those of ancient times, "You shall not murder"'; and "whoever murders shall be liable to judgment." But I say to you that if you are angry with a brother or sister, you will be liable to judgment; and if you insult a brother or sister, you will be liable to the council; and if you say, "You fool," you will be liable to the hell of fire. So when you are offering your gift at the altar, if you remember that your brother or sister has something against you, leave your gift there before the altar and go; first be reconciled to your brother or sister, and then come and offer your gift. (Matthew 5;21-25)

Spiritual decluttering involves discarding everything that prevents us from experiencing God's presence in ourselves and in our neighbors. Jesus' words are easily misunderstood. Jesus is not denying the reality of anger and situations that deserve our righteous indignation. Certain types of anger can be beneficial when they protect us and others from harm or injustice. Jesus was righteously indignant at those who saw the temple as a place of business rather than prayer. He fiercely challenged those who excluded persons from God's realm based on health condition, ethnicity, gender, and social standing. Anger can motivate us to transform our communities and nation. There is a holy anger we experience when time after time our political leaders fail to act in the wake of another mass shooting of children and youth. We can be prophetically irate at policies that place the planet and our grandchildren in jeopardy for the sake of short-term profit. We can energetically challenge political leaders who threaten nuclear war as if its playground competition. Such anger is based on God's passion for justice and reverence for life. The prophetic anger of Jesus and the Hebraic prophets may have felt harsh toward those who were at the receiving end, but it is grounded on love for the offender as well as the offended. They channeled their anger so that it became a force in changing unhealthy relationships and business and governmental practices.

Still, we know that festering anger, like habitual stress, can ruin our health and relationships. Anger is a feeling, a response to a threat, an injustice, or a personal insult. As such, it has a role in social change and self-affirmation. But, holding onto anger or stoking the flames of anger, as we see on talk radio or among certain politicians, alienates us from God and each other. It puts us on high alert, when we need calm to make good decisions for ourselves and others.

There is great wisdom in the words of Ephesians 4:26: "Be angry but do not sin; do not let the sun go down on your anger." Anger can motivate us to change the world and protect the innocent and bullied. This anger is intended to be beneficial, and healthy responses to anger involve letting go of negative emotions once they no longer serve a higher purpose. "Do not let the sun go down on your anger." In other words, don't hold onto it. Let your grievances be known in an appropriate fashion, remembering that those with whom you are angry are also God's children and that sometimes our anger is misplaced or misdirected.

Jesus counsels us to self-awareness and reconciliation. When you are angry, take a moment to gain spiritual perspective with a few deep breaths. Notice the feelings and reflect on their source to discern if your anger is justified, appropriate and healthy. Act on your anger, if the situation requires it, and then to the best of your ability, place your anger in God's care, for God to shape it in ways that are healthy for you and others. Discard the clutter of harmful and unnecessary anger so God's healing energy and compassion can flow through you.

Prayerful Decluttering. Spiritual decluttering involves mindfulness or self-awareness. Be aware of your moods throughout the day, registering any feelings of resentment, alienation, or anger. Note the emotions without judgment, and without over-intellectualizing try to discern their immediate source. Prayerfully consider how to respond to your anger in a way that is healthy for you and those around you.

Prayerfully ask God: "God of justice and reconciliation, help me to experience your presence in my anger. Help me to use my passions for good and not for evil, for justice and not revenge. Help me to let go of all that separates me from my brothers and sisters. Amen."

A Simple Practice: If you identify times when your anger has hurt others, ask God to help you find a way to make amends and seek forgiveness. Sometimes seeking forgiveness is neither possible or advisable. In that case, place your regret in God's care for God to bring the healing to a relationship. In like manner, ask God to help you forgive those who you believe have harmed you. Place your anger in God's care, asking God to guide you to healing and wholeness in difficult relationships.

Day Twenty-Five
A World without Enemies

You have heard that it was said, 'You shall love your neighbor and hate your enemy.' But I say to you, Love your enemies and pray for those who persecute you, so that you may be children of your Father in heaven; for he makes his sun rise on the evil and on the good, and sends rain on the righteous and on the unrighteous... Be perfect, therefore, as your heavenly Father is perfect. (Matthew 5:43-45, 48)

Jesus challenged us to be "perfect" as God is perfect. In this passage, Jesus is not denying that good people will make mistakes or commit sins in their relationships. We may even hold grudges that eventually we need to prune for our own spiritual growth. Some theological and biblical commentators believe that "perfection" means "whole" or "inclusive." God's love is all-embracing and calls us to be all-embracing as well. Persons of spiritual stature go beyond "insider" and "outsider" and "friend" and "enemy." They see holiness even in those with whom they disagree. They see God's image not only in the "least of these," but the "worst of these." A life of spiritual simplicity looks for God in all God's hidden disguises. Spiritual stature means letting go of the cumber of resentment, so we can enjoy the fullness of love.

I deal with my own temptation to polarize by praying for those whose words and behaviors appall and alienate me, including national leaders and cable news commentators as well as thoughtless drivers or shoppers. In my own quest for spiritual and relational simplicity, I seek to bless everyone I meet or view on the news, even when I must challenge their behaviors and viewpoints. I try to follow the vision of poet Edwin Markham:

He drew a circle who shut me out
Heretic, rebel, thing to flout
But love and I had the wit to win:
We drew a circle that took him in!

Prayerful Decluttering. Take a spiritual inventory today. Did you get mad today? Was your anger related to a friend or stranger, or a public figure? Whom are your personal enemies? Who do you love to hate? In what ways do your enmities make your life more complex and diminish your quality of life? In what ways can you prune away the polarizing detritus of your life?

Pray for your enemies as follows: "God of all peoples, help me draw circles of love that include those with whom I disagree; help me let go of grievances, even as I challenge policies and viewpoints they may hold. Amen."

A Spiritual Practice. Jesus tells us that we are the light of the world and to let our light shine. Let you light shine on those whom you are tempted to brand as enemies. Visualize God's radiant wisdom and love filling their hearts and minds and guiding them toward God's Shalom. While you may disagree with such persons, you can still see the light in them and let go of any animosity toward them, trusting that God will guide them to wholeness. If these persons are in your circle of acquaintances, ask for God's guidance to find a way to move from alienation to care, even if you still are uncomfortable in their presence. Is there one act that can cut away the clutter of resentment so you can feel the calm of healthy relatedness?

Day Twenty-Six
Beyond Self-interest

Our Father in heaven,
hallowed be your name.
Your kingdom come.
Your will be done,
on earth as it is in heaven. (Matthew 5:9-10)

Philosopher Alfred North Whitehead describes the experience of peace as the result of letting go of your ego and identifying with the well-being of others. No longer imprisoned by the fearful, anxious, and isolated self, we experience ourselves as connected with the whole universe in a dynamic web of relatedness. What is good for others, in terms of their highest good, becomes good for us. Grounded in a sense of God's abundance, we can sacrifice for others' well-being without experiencing emotional, spiritual, or economic loss. We can simplify our lives by letting go of competition and envy and seeking the highest good – God's blessing and healing – for strangers as well as friends.

The Lord's Prayer invites us to align ourselves with God's all-embracing love. God's vision becomes our vision, God's quest for Shalom becomes our quest, as we let God guide our steps. "Your kingdom come. Your will be done, on earth as it is in heaven." In aligning ourselves with God's realm, we are no longer buffeted around by competing emotions, but have the peace of "doing one thing," bringing God's wisdom and care to every situation.

Prayerful Decluttering. The philosopher Soren Kierkegaard asserted that "purity of heart is to will one thing." While God wants to expand our freedom and creativity, congruent with the greatest good for ourselves and others, we find our deepest joy in aligning ourselves with God's will in every situation.

Throughout the day, ask God, "What is your will – your vision – in this situation?" and then listen, trusting that God will move within your life in each life situation.

A Simple Practice. As you live with the Lord's Prayer, especially the phrase, "Your will be done on earth as it is in heaven," what one thing is God calling you toward today?" How might you might you embody God's will in your daily life? In what ways does following God's will open you to new horizons of possibility and provide guidance in your process of spiritual decluttering?

Day Twenty-Seven
Beyond Consumerism

Do not store up for yourselves treasures on earth, where moth and rust consume and where thieves break in and steal; but store up for yourselves treasures in heaven, where neither moth nor rust consumes and where thieves do not break in and steal. For where your treasure is, there your heart will be also. (Matthew 6:19-21)

What is most important to you? What do you really want out of life? What truly satisfies your spirit? Over the years, I have been pastor to many affluent youth and adults. From the world's perspective, they had everything – expensive homes and cars, the ability to travel, power, prestige – but many of them lacked a sense of meaning and purpose. They had gained the whole world but had lost their souls. They had difficulty sustaining healthy relationships and, in some cases, were diagnosed with chronic and life-threatening illnesses that money could not cure. Wealth and power cannot purchase joy or peace of mind that comes from an ongoing relationship with God.

What are "treasures in heaven?" What endures through the passage of time? Jesus' way of life roots meaning and purpose in our relationships with God, one another. Meaning emerges from our sense of spiritual wholeness and willingness to sacrifice for a greater good. Our ceaseless consumption reflects our quest for wholeness, albeit often in destructive and unsatisfying ways. We want to fill a void that can only be addressed through the love of God and others. The apostle Paul asserts that "love never ends." (I Corinthians 13:8) Despite the positive benefits of a certain level of affluence, the greatest treasures of love arise from healthy relationships, good work, meaningful service, self-acceptance, and care for the broader community.

"Where our treasure is, our heart is." The dubious treasures we seek have led to ecological destruction, the growing gap between the rich and poor, unfaithful relationships, frenetic schedules to support our buying habits, and focusing on things rather than presence in our relationships. The "seven deadly sins," especially greed, lust, and envy, have become socially acceptable and are touted in commercials, political policies, and marketing campaigns. In contrast, spiritual decluttering reminds us that "less" can be "more" in terms of contentment and joy. As German mystic Meister Eckhardt asserts, we know God by subtraction, by diminishing what stands between God and us, rather than by adding possessions, titles, or even doctrines. Our practices of spiritual decluttering help us prune away and discard our false attempts to find fulfillment and enables us to experience, perhaps for the first time, our own deep creativity and goodness and the beauty of life around us. Nothing can destroy the beauty of love, the spirit of creativity, the holiness of sacrifice. These treasures, born of choosing to love the Creator in our relationship will all God's creation, last forever.

Prayerful Decluttering. In the spirit of the Examen or examination of conscience, consider the following scenario: Your home is on fire and you've rushed outside to preserve your life. You discover that you have left something important inside. What would you return to retrieve? What the true treasures that you would risk your life to save? What really matters?

Let us pray: "Show me, Giver of beauty and love, my true treasures, and let this vision guide my decisions about time, talent, and treasure. Amen."

A Simple Practice. Building on today's prayerful decluttering exercise, notice the difference between ultimate and penultimate treasures. To gain lasting treasures, we may have to give up lesser treasures, important but not all-important, good but not necessary. While these reflections may inspire you to further declutter your office, study, or home, they can also give you a sense of what is expendable in your life, so that you can let go of certain attachments to experience true treasures. You can put these material and emotional attachments in your "spiritual decluttering" container either to give away or prune from your personal life.

Day Twenty-Eight
Beyond Anxiety

> *Therefore I tell you, do not worry about your life, what you*
> *will eat or what you will drink, or about your body, what you*
> *will wear. Is not life more than food, and the body more than*
> *clothing? Look at the birds of the air; they neither sow nor reap*
> *nor gather into barns, and yet your heavenly Father feeds them.*
> *Are you not of more value than they? And can any of you by*
> *worrying add a single hour to your span of life? And why do you*
> *worry about clothing? Consider the lilies of the field, how they*
> *grow; they neither toil nor spin, yet I tell you, even Solomon in all*
> *his glory was not clothed like one of these. But if God so clothes the*
> *grass of the field, which is alive today and tomorrow is thrown into*
> *the oven, will he not much more clothe you—you of little faith?...*
> *and indeed your heavenly Father knows that you need all these*
> *things. But strive first for the kingdom of God and his righteous-*
> *ness, and all these things will be given to you as well." So do not*
> *worry about tomorrow, for tomorrow will bring worries of its own.*
> *Today's trouble is enough for today.* (Matthew 6:25-30, 32b-34)

Can we trust God to respond to our deepest needs? That is the central question of faith. This is true today, and it was equally true in the prescientific, slow-moving days of Jesus' ministry. Jesus assures his followers and assures us that God cares for the least as well as the greatest. Divine providence cares for the birds of the air and the grasses of the field, and divine providence cares for us.

Like a good parent, God provides for our ultimate security and success. We need to trust that when everything has failed us, God will come through. God will supply our needs! God's promise, however, challenges us to discern what we truly need and what is truly important for our well-being. A psychotherapist friend of mine posted the following message on his home phone, "Please leave a message telling me who you are and what you want?" and then added "Be careful how you answer the question. It might just surprise you." In affirming God's providential care, Jesus is also asking us to examine our own lives. According to a recent study, once people achieve a certain level of income, roughly $100,000, any amount beyond that sum does not add to their happiness. The quest for financial security and personal gain can lead to greater emotional and relational cumber, and not enduring joy and peace of mind.

In the spirit of Maslow's hierarchy of values, we need to ensure that everyone has adequate shelter, income, food, education, and possibility for personal growth. One of the tragedies of poverty and powerlessness is that it stunts the imagination of children. They expect "less" rather than "more" out of life and of themselves. Our responsibility as persons of privilege is that the marginalized and dispossessed have sufficient resources to awaken their imaginations and sense of possibility and agency. When we trust God to supply our deepest needs, then we can joyfully sacrifice, and even downsize, to promote the well-being of others. When we seek first God's realm, we will, as Jesus says, have everything we need.

Spiritual Decluttering. Once again, prayerfully explore the relationship between what you "want" and what you "need" to be fulfilled. Let the distance between wants and needs guide your home economics and decision-making and inspire you to dispense with activities and possessions that create anxiety and overly complicate our lives. We may discover that our lifestyles unnecessarily create anxiety, requiring us to work harder and longer and spend less time on meaningful activities and relationships with loved ones.

Let us surround ourselves in prayer: "God of abundant life, help me to trust your providential abundance and share out my largesse gifts of time, talent, and treasure to upbuild my community. Amen."

A Simple Practice. Once more, look at your material needs and possessions. As a spiritual practice, let go of one thing you no longer need, by discarding, recycling, or giving to a local thrift shop or community service program.

WEEK FIVE

CALL AND RESPONSE

Spiritual decluttering is grounded in a dynamic process of call and response. God calls and we respond, and our response opens the door to new possibilities for God and ourselves. We are never powerless to change ourselves or our communities when we awaken to God's providence in our lives. Within what we perceive to be the limitations of life, God provides a plethora of possibilities. Concreteness is the womb of possibility, and when we trust God, we will discover the wisdom of Philippians 4:19: "my God will fully satisfy every need of yours according to his riches in glory in Christ Jesus."

Day Twenty-Nine
Beyond Judgment

> *Do not judge, so that you may not be judged. For with the judgment you make you will be judged, and the measure you give will be the measure you get. Why do you see the speck in your neighbor's eye, but do not notice the log in your own eye? Or how can you say to your neighbor, "Let me take the speck out of your eye," while the log is in your own eye?* (Matthew 7:1-4)

Many of us constantly judge ourselves and others. We have an inner voice that constantly measures us against some scale of perfection, in relationship to which we always far short. Our self-talk is negative and limiting. Moreover, in judging ourselves in relationship with others, we inevitably fall short of their achievements, or at least we expend unnecessary energy trying to keep up with those around us. The same standards we apply to ourselves we also apply to others. We build walls of judgment on others based on their appearance, class, race, gender and sexuality, and political viewpoints. Despite the fact that judgment may give us temporary feelings of moral, intellectual, spiritual superiority, judgment always separates us from others and from God. When we feel judgment on ourselves from God or others, the seeds of low self-esteem are planted. We need to justify ourselves, protesting our moral or spiritual integrity. In the process, life becomes a competition, a battle in which others must lose in order for me to feel adequate.

There is another way, the way of spiritual simplicity, in which I begin by accepting my life and others simply as they are. Self-acceptance doesn't mean denial or giving up on excellence; it simply means that I embrace the whole of my life, positive and negative, as an opportunity for growth, healing, and adventure. Accepting others, likewise, means seeing the holiness within them, oft-hidden by external behaviors, and recognizing that they too are in process of growth, finite and limited and yet God's beloved children. When we begin with acceptance, we can face life as it is in all its wondrous messiness.

We can enjoy the present moment and recognize that we may still have a long way to go. Fifty years ago, Thomas Anthony Harris proclaimed "I'm ok, you're ok," as a necessary first step to personal growth. In response, Elizabeth Kubler Ross penned, "I'm not ok, and you're not ok, but it's ok." Both sentiments are correct. Right now, we are enough! Right now, we can rejoice in our unique personality. Kubler-Ross' rejoinder reminds us that as imperfect as we are, we are loved by God and valued as God's beloved child. In either case, we don't have to justify ourselves, prove our worth, or diminish others to feel good about ourselves. The simplicity of a non-judgmental life allows us to recognize both the positive and negative, without succumbing to envy, hate, or alienation. We are "ok" even when we aren't as God's beloved children.

Spiritual Decluttering. Devote today to mindfulness. Observe your tendencies to judge yourself or others. What do you judge in others? What self-talk do you use for yourself and others? How does this self-talk shape your attitudes toward self and others? As you observe your judgmentalism, consider whether or not it is warranted or helpful in your quest for wholeness.

Let this be your prayer: "Deliver me, O God, from judgment so that I might see others and myself as we are, holy, imperfect, and loved. Amen."

A Simple Practice. Focus on your language as well as your thoughts. Do your best to eliminate judgmental language from your interactions. Take off the lens of judgment in relationship to others. Let your speech be neutral or positive. Challenge persons with "I-statements" rather than abstract judgments or character attacks.

Day Thirty
Calling on God

Ask, and it will be given you; search, and you will find; knock, and the door will be opened for you. For everyone who asks receives, and everyone who searches finds, and for everyone who knocks, the door will be opened. (Matthew 7:7-8)

Could it be that God always answers our prayers, but we just don't notice it? British pastor Leslie Weatherhead once asserted that "when I pray, coincidences happen, and when I don't, they don't." Jesus counsel in the Sermon on the Mount is an invitation to reflect on our spiritual quest by asking the questions: "For what do I ask from God? For what am I searching? On what door am I knocking?" How we answer these questions will shape our prayers and self-awareness and help us discern our deepest desires hidden beneath the multitude of desires that vie for our attention.

The quest for spiritual simplicity begins with the asking. What truly great request do you want to receive from God? In a way, this is a bit like the wishes of Aladdin's lamp. Many people waste their wishes – their energy, their time – on trivial things, and forget to ask for the one thing they truly need.

Then comes the searching. Do you remember the song by the Irish band U-2 "I still haven't found what I'm looking?" The search may take us, as it does the rock band, to the highest mountains and to healing finger tips. The adventure of spiritual growth is unending but we can find places of wholeness and purpose on the way.

The quest continues with knocking, that is, reaching out to others or choosing certain paths to find your spiritual fulfillment. Upon whose door might you knock to receive help to realize your audacious request.

The path toward God's vision for us is both solitary and relational. We need to let God's vision grow within us and we also need to reach out to wise women and men, to resources in our midst, and to our Companion God.

Prayerful Decluttering. "Ask, search, knock." Sometimes we need to ask for what we need to ask to find God's vision for us. First, we need to reflect on what we truly need. What are we truly looking for and how will we go about getting it? Let this day call you to prayer for guidance and the wisdom to let go of the extraneous so that the divine road may rise up to greet you.

Let your day be guided by the prayer: "Be with me in my asking, guide me in my searching, energize me in my knocking. Amen."

A Simple Practice: Decluttering means pruning the extraneous. The word "decision" means to cut off. Every road taken eliminates another pathway, at least for the moment. We may need to leave the broad thoroughfares to discover ourselves on "the road less traveled." (Robert Frost) Are there any paths that you need to reject to experience abundant life? Let me share from my own life. I grew up early, as a child of the summer of love I was using marijuana, hashish, opium, and LSD by my mid-teens. I was on a spiritual quest, not just a hedonistic party. In my first year of college, I decided that this path no longer served me. Though I was not addicted, I knew that I needed to find another way. So, one October Saturday in 1980, I entered an ashram, a spiritual center, where I learned Transcendental Meditation. In learning to meditate, I left the world of drugs and never looked back, even though it cost me some friends. In the process of learning

*to meditate, I rediscovered Jesus as companion and guide and entered
that pathway that led me to ministry and teaching.*

Day Thirty-One
God is Calling on You

> *Listen! I am standing at the door, knocking; if you hear my
> voice and open the door, I will come in to you and eat with you,
> and you with me.* (Revelation 3:20)

God is looking for you! God is not absent or faraway but as
near as your next breath. God's heart beats with yours and God's
Spirit breathes within your spirit. God prays within us even when
we don't have a prayer of our own and God brings persons and
events into our lives to help us find our way.

Our spiritual life, even when we are unaware of it, is a dynamic
process of call and response. God is constantly calling to us. God's
whispered word is constantly trying to get our attention. "God is
still speaking," as the United Church of Christ affirms. But, are
we listening? There is no one path to listening for God's presence
or opening the door to the Holy Stranger. Perhaps, we can find
guidance from the poet Mary Oliver, who spends an afternoon
transfixed by a grasshopper going about its business unaware of
her vigil "I don't know exactly what a prayer is. I do know how to
pay attention."[6]

Pay attention. Listen for God's knock at the door of your heart
and then welcome God in as your companion in this wonderful
and tragic life. You will find meaning and purpose, and every day
will become a holy adventure.

*Prayerful Decluttering. It has been said that we find God by
subtraction. In other words, we hear God knocking at our door, when
we silence the inner and outer din. We have a love affair with noise in
our society. Some of it is beautiful and good, but virtually everywhere*

---

6   Mary Oliver, "The Summer Day."

you go, there is background music, a newsfeed, or sports or news on television. As Paul Simon says, we need to listen for the sounds of silence to hear God's still, small voice. Prophets can address us anywhere, even in the words of prophetic street artists. "written on subway walls and tenement halls." Be still in the maelstrom. Take time for a "time out" to listen throughout the day: pause, take a few breaths, notice what's going on in your life, look beneath the surface for the whispered word of God, as theologian Marjorie Suchocki counsels. What is the rhythm of divine knocking? Who is there when you open the door? What pathway rises up to meet you?

Let your prayer be: "Loving God, help me turn of the background noise, the monkey mind, so I can hear the sounds of silence and discern your prophetic word. Give me courage to hear and then respond, taking my role in God's holy adventure. Amen."

A Simple Practice. I have a Google Personal Assistant, a relative of the Amazon Alexa. Sometimes when I ask my assistant to play a song, the volume is almost deafening. I have to respond, "OK, Google, please lower the volume." We all need to lower the volume so we can listen to the voice of God. Try to speak in a lower, calmer voice and then pause to listen, without comment, before you respond. Turn off your various sound sources – radio, television, MP3, etc. – to enjoy the silence. Perhaps, with young Samuel, from the biblical story, we can respond, "Speak, God, I'm listening."

Day Thirty-Two
A House on the Rock

Everyone then who hears these words of mine and acts on them will be like a wise man who built his house on rock. The rain fell, the floods came, and the winds blew and beat on that house, but it did not fall, because it had been founded on rock. And everyone who hears these words of mine and does not act on them will be like a foolish man who built his house on sand. The rain fell, and the floods came, and the winds blew and beat against that house, and it fell—and great was its fall!" (Matthew 7:24-27)

Is your house built on a rock? In my native California, luxurious homes are often constructed on mountain sides. When heavy rains, it is not uncommon for a house to slide down the hill or be washed into the sea because it did not have sufficient foundation to withstand the storm. Simplicity of life involves coming to know the difference between the dependable and the untrustworthy. Such discernment may be a matter of life and death on the hillside, the highway, and in our daily lives and spiritual decision-making.

Jesus asks "Who do you trust when the going gets tough? Have you built your life upon the rock of fidelity or the sands of uncertainty?" Theologian Paul Tillich speaks of the God who emerges when all the other gods – the gods of our own making – have collapsed. Even the best of us worship "golden calves" from time to time. We focus our energies and devote ourselves to the unsubstantial and believe the false promises of advertisers, politicians, spiritual entrepreneurs, and get rich con artists. Spiritual growth takes time, but the journey is worth it. We need soul food not fast food, solid construction and not quick fixes, solid ground and not shifting stands. Plant your feet on solid rock, the rock of God's salvation, which delivers today and promises hope for tomorrow.

Prayerful Decluttering. Is your house build on the rock? Look at your life and your surroundings. What things are insubstantial and flimsy, quick but superficial? Consider, at an appropriate time, to discard flimsy furniture and worthless products. Consider eliminating insubstantial activities from your life.

Let us pray together: "Holy One, help me to build the house of life on solid rock. Give me a spirit of discernment, able to go beyond the superficial to the enduring. Amen."

A Simple Practice. We hear a lot about "fake news" these days. We also hear about "false values." Examine your news consumption, whether on the internet or television. How does it shape your life? Do you know if your sources are accurate or propaganda? Do you make decisions based on reflection or emotion, when it comes to your politi-

cal opinions? Seek to discern the difference between the wheat and the chaff in the media and politics. Try to prune away media that inflame, antagonize, or raise your anxiety level.

Day Thirty-Three
Loaves and Fish

> *When he looked up and saw a large crowd coming toward him, Jesus said to Philip, "Where are we to buy bread for these people to eat?" He said this to test him, for he himself knew what he was going to do. Philip answered him, "Six months' wages would not buy enough bread for each of them to get a little." One of his disciples, Andrew, Simon Peter's brother, said to him, "There is a boy here who has five barley loaves and two fish. But what are they among so many people?" Jesus said, "Make the people sit down." Now there was a great deal of grass in the place; so they sat down, about five thousand in all. Then Jesus took the loaves, and when he had given thanks, he distributed them to those who were seated; so also the fish, as much as they wanted. When they were satisfied, he told his disciples, "Gather up the fragments left over, so that nothing may be lost." (John 5:6-12)*

Spiritual simplicity is ironically about "more" rather than "less." It is about a different kind of "more" than our culture promises. When we simplify our lives, we often move from scarcity thinking to abundant living. Spiritual decluttering leads to more personal time, more creativity, more recreation, and more time with loved ones. We may even discover that we have more money to spend on experiences we value and causes that benefit our planet and persons in need.

Scripture proclaims that a little child shall lead them, and in this Gospel story a little child does! A little boy incarnates a central principle of the realm of God, the growth of a mustard seed into a great plant. He trusts God's bounty as he gives up his lunch for the well-being of a great crowd. While we don't need to understand the mechanics of the miracle of feeding of the five thousand, there are at least two miraculous explanations: Jesus multiplied the loaves and fish by focusing the divine creative energy of the world, the natural miracle powers of nature, or the boy's generosity and Jesus' message inspired the five thousand gathered to move from scarcity to abundance and let go of their strangle hold on the lunches they brought. Either way a miracle occurred and the hungry were fed!

I have found that when I let go of my grip on my time, talent, or treasure, I end up having more than I previously anticipated. In moving from scarcity thinking to abundant living, new energies are released and my life becomes spacious when previously it was cramped. I have learned to live by the biblical promise, "my God will fully satisfy every need of yours according to his riches in glory in Christ Jesus." (Philippians 4:19)   Even in challenging times, and this is not magic or materialistic "prosperity gospel" thinking, God will supply. There is always enough to go around when we are willing to share. The hungry are fed, the poor have health care, the homeless find shelter.

Prayerful Decluttering. Today, we need to take steps to discard thoughts of limitation and scarcity. Consider for a moment the question, "What are your five loaves and two fish?" or "What are your resources in time, talent, and treasure?" How do you feel about your resources? Do you feel limited or abundant? This is often a matter of perception. For example, during the American Depression of the 1930's many people going through hard times helped each other out. They shared with their neighbors, they extended credit for groceries, they lowered rental fees. Looking back many of these depression families make the affirmation, "we weren't poor, we just didn't have any money." They experienced abundance despite their apparently scarce circumstances. In that same spirit, when we open our hearts to divine abundance, we discover that God's "power at work within us is able to accomplish abundantly far more than all we can ask or imagine." (Ephesians 3:20)

Let us pray, and let your prayer include other readers unknown to you: "Let your power flow through me to bring joy and abundance to everyone around me. Amen."

A Simple Practice. Today, in all the circumstances of life, repeat the affirmation, "I have all the time, talent, and treasure to accomplish everything I need to flourish and serve God and humankind" or "God is able to accomplish in and through me more than I can ask or imagine."

Day Thirty-Four
Safety in the Storm

> *On that day, when evening had come, he said to them, "Let us go across to the other side." And leaving the crowd behind, they took him with them in the boat, just as he was. Other boats were with him. A great windstorm arose, and the waves beat into the boat, so that the boat was already being swamped. But he was in the stern, asleep on the cushion; and they woke him up and said to him, "Teacher, do you not care that we are perishing?" He woke up and rebuked the wind, and said to the sea, "Peace! Be still!" Then the wind ceased, and there was a dead calm. He said to them, "Why are you afraid? Have you still no faith?"* (Mark 4:35-40)

There are times when we feel buffeted by the storms of life. We wonder if they will swamp our spirits. As the Cape Cod saying goes, "the sea is so wide and my boat is so small." Problems loom large and our resources seem meager by comparison. Dwarfed by the challenges of life, we often are overwhelmed by anxiety and seek to still the storm by alcohol, drugs, work, consumerism, and even religion. We seek to find ways to control reality, and if not that, deny or narcotize ourselves so we will not feel the pain of life.

The story of Jesus and the storm at sea is a reminder that even when God seems absent, God is with us quietly present with us in the storm. In the spirit of the poem, "Footprints," those moments when we see only one set of footprints on the sand, God is carrying us, ensuring our ultimate well-being.

Faith involves a lively, reckless confidence in God's grace, as Martin Luther is reputed to have said. Faith trusts that there is a deeper power at work in our lives and the world than we are currently seeing. When we place our trust in God, letting go of our futile need to control reality and place our lives in God's care, new energies emerge and new possibilities surface. Faith in God's care, fully relying on God's grace, ironically gives us greater power and agency than when we think falsely that we can go it alone. When we trust God in the storms of life, we discover that there is but one source of our safety and salvation. We no longer live in a fractured world of false and competing demigods but live courageously knowing that God's love will companion and care for us. Confident in God's care, we can choose rightly and live simply.

Prayerful Decluttering. Author Anne Lamott asserts that prayer involves the three movements of "wow," "thanks," and "help." All three movements reflect our awareness that our lives are in the care of a wisdom, power, and love greater than our own. Today, experiment with praying for help. Throughout the day, recognize those situations in which you must let go of control or where your knowledge and ability is incomplete and you need greater energy and insight. give me wisdom." Then, wait for God's response as you pray: "Help me, O God, trust your wisdom. Guide my path. Give me guidance for every new step. Amen."

A Simple Practice. Throughout the day, imagine that Jesus is beside you in every encounter. In the spirit of Celtic Christian spirituality, you may choose the practice of "caim" or "encircling," as you say part of a prayer attributed to St. Patrick:

> *Christ with me, Christ before me, Christ behind me,*
> *Christ in me, Christ beneath me, Christ above me,*
> *Christ on my right, Christ on my left,*
> *Christ when I lie down, Christ when I sit down,*
> *Christ in the heart of everyone who thinks of me,*
> *Christ in the mouth of everyone who speaks of me,*

Christ in the eye that sees me,
Christ in the ear that hears me.

Day Thirty-Five
Looking to Jesus

Peter answered him, "Lord, if it is you, command me to come to you on the water." He said, "Come." So Peter got out of the boat, started walking on the water, and came toward Jesus. But when he noticed the strong wind, he became frightened, and beginning to sink, he cried out, "Lord, save me!" Jesus immediately reached out his hand and caught him, saying to him, "You of little faith, why did you doubt?" When they got into the boat, the wind ceased. (Matthew 14:28-32)

Keep your eyes on Jesus! The object of our trust, the focus of our thoughts, can save or harm us. In a companion to the story of the storm at sea, Peter takes a leap of faith into the stormy sea. Everything is going well – to his amazement he is walking on water – until he turns away from Jesus. In that split second, he begins to sink.

Simplicity of spirit comes when we focus our attention on Jesus, or a meaningful symbol of spiritual wholeness. Eyes on Jesus, we can turn away from the temptations of false gods – consumption, material goods, success, power, and control – toward the authentic source of wholeness. We can visualize our spiritual journey as walking toward Jesus or following his path. One of my favorite hymns is a hymn originating among the Christians of India, where turning toward Jesus could mean losing your standing in the community or being disinherited by your family.

I have decided to follow Jesus;
I have decided to follow Jesus;
I have decided to follow Jesus;
No turning back, no turning back.

The world behind me, the cross before me;
The world behind me, the cross before me;
The world behind me, the cross before me;
No turning back, no turning back.

Though none go with me, still I will follow;
Though none go with me, still I will follow;
Though none go with me, still I will follow;
No turning back, no turning back.

Following Jesus does not require us to disparage other paths or deny their validity as God-inspired paths of salvation. Keeping your eyes on Jesus and following his path serves as the horizon toward which we travel throughout the day. With eyes on Jesus, we can discern what is important and unimportant or valuable or worthless. Eyes on Jesus, our spiritual GPS guides us through the maze of daily lives.

Prayerful Decluttering. Once again, we take an adventure in self-awareness, focusing on the twin questions, "What takes our eyes off Jesus?" and "What enables us to focus on Jesus?" when our eyes are on Jesus, we do "only one thing" amid our many activities, see Jesus and follow his guidance in the many events of everyday life. Some activities and thought patterns obviously alienate us from God, while others deepen our focus on Jesus. As you consider what takes your eyes off Jesus, make a commitment to be mindful of these unhealthy distractions so that you can return to Jesus as soon as possible after your focus is confused. Jesus is always there to pull you out of the raging waters.

Pray throughout the day: "God of wind and waves, reorient my spiritual GPS so that my eyes be turned toward you. Give me focus to stay on the path and courage to let go of anything that hides your presence from me. Amen."

A Simple Practice. As you consider what tempts you to take your eyes off Jesus, make a commitment to eliminate any external temptations. These could revolve on an overly booked schedule, your inability to say "no," inappropriate relationships, or a house whose clutter requires you to spend unnecessary time or money for upkeep or cleaning.

Do your best to discard one of these temptations while also beginning to let go of thought patterns that create anxiety, fear, or lack of focus.

Week Six

Grace and Gratitude

A recent New York Times article noted that saying "thank you" is becoming a lost art, especially among younger Americans and counseled the practice of "counting your blessings." The German mystic Meister Eckhardt asserted that "if the only prayer you make is 'thank you,' that will be enough." Gratitude grounds us in the graceful interdependence and reminds us that our largesse and privilege is the gift of God, the world around us, our family of origin, and personal and professional support from friends, colleagues, and mentors. Rugged individualism and the ingratitude that goes with it shrinks our world and makes others' success a threat to our own. When we are grateful, we experience abundance despite the limitations of life. I have tried on a daily basis with a song I learned in my childhood Baptist church:

> When upon life's billows you are tempest-tossed,
> When you are discouraged, thinking all is lost,
> Count your many blessings, name them one by one,
> And it will surprise you what the Lord has done.
> Count your blessings, name them one by one,
> Count your blessings, see what God has done!
> Count your blessings, name them one by one,
> Count your many blessings, see what God has done.

An "attitude of gratitude" can transform your life, set your priorities, and enable you to experience true simplicity in a complex world.

Day Thirty-Six
Be Transformed

Do not be conformed to this world, but be transformed by the renewing of your minds, so that you may discern what is the will of God—what is good and acceptable and perfect. (Romans 12:2)

We are all creatures of our unique culture, family of origin, communities, time and place. Many of our values come from the larger world and despite the claim of many that America is a Christian nation, compassion, simplicity, and generosity are often trumped by greed, individualism, and consumption. Often, we prize success and power over healthy relationships and spiritual growth. This is not just true of the United States but of virtually every culture and nation in the developed world. In contrast, the spirit of simplicity challenges us to be countercultural and to embrace the values of sharing, gratitude, family life, and sacrifice. These are the values that endure and bring healing to our families and communities.

Spiritual teachers proclaim that transformation is possible. We can let go of values that no longer serve our best interest or the well-being of our communities and the planet and embrace new values that to the love and beauty of the world. In embracing new values, we cut through the clutter of life and begin to discern "the will of God – what is good and perfect and acceptable."

Prayerful Decluttering. Spiritual decluttering is a lifelong journey. The values of our culture are powerful and threaten to undermine our resolve to live more simply and care more deeply. We are tempted to build walls to protect us from diverse people and opinions. Every day we receive images of consumption that identify happiness with ownership, whether of a new automobile, furniture, or home. We are told that happiness comes from financial security, whiter teeth, or a trim waist. There is nothing wrong with these, provided that we remember that what truly matters are our relationship with God, our love of friends and family, our commitment to the well-being of our communities, and our willingness to sacrifice for the survival of future generations of humans and non-human. In a time of spiritual examination, consider your greatest temptations. Where are you most likely to "conform" to the world? In what ways might you experience the transformation grounded in an alternative set of values?

Let this be your prayer: "Let me trust your providence, let it shape my values, and let me hopefully await the glorious harvest you have in store for me and the world through my commitments. Amen."

A Simple Practice. Based on the previous spiritual exercise, look at your current life, considering where your "conforming to the world" is evident in your daily life. What one activity or thought pattern can you discard to be more faithful to God's vision for you and the world?

Day Thirty-Seven
God's Good Work Will Continue

> *I thank my God every time I remember you, constantly pray-ing with joy in every one of my prayers for all of you, because of your sharing in the gospel from the first day until now. I am con-fident of this, that the one who began a good work among you will bring it to completion by the day of Jesus Christ…And this is my prayer, that your love may overflow more and more with knowledge and full insight to help you to determine what is best, so that in the day of Christ you may be pure and blameless, having produced the harvest of righteousness that comes through Jesus Christ for the glory and praise of God.* (Philippians 1:3-6, 9-11)

A wise spiritual guide once said that the spiritual journey is a continual process of falling down and getting back up again. Our best resolutions are often forgotten amid conflicting voices and values of our society and our own personal dramas. At times, we feel guilt and shame at how far we've strayed from our highest values and how easy it is to turn from God's vision for our lives. Old patterns have power, and the past can overwhelm us in its pain and familiarity. But, we have the promise that God is at work in our lives and that good work God has begun in us will come to fulfillment.

The road to simplicity of spirit is paved by divine providence. God is working in our lives, guiding our steps, presenting us with possibilities, placing situations and persons in our lives, and challenging our assumptions. Trusting God's providence enables us to separate the "wheat from the chaff" in our lives. The more we open to God's wisdom and creativity, the more energy, focus, and direction we have in our lives. Just taking the first step in openness to God will awaken a world of wonders and possibility for you. God is with you, giving you everything you need to let go of the past and open to a glorious future.

Spiritual Decluttering. In this decluttering practice, train your senses for God moments throughout the day. Open to providential encounters, insights, and intuitions and then ask for God's guidance to provide the wisdom to respond.

Let us pray: "Holy One, open my senses, heart, and mind to moments of grace and inspiration, and let me follow your vision of abundant life for myself and the world around me. Amen."

A Simple Practice. With open eyes and hands, seize a God moment in the day ahead. Follow the guidance you are receiving and see what happens when you trust God's providence working in your life.

Day Thirty-Eight
Giving Thanks

Rejoice in the Lord always; again I will say, Rejoice. Let your gentleness be known to everyone. The Lord is near. Do not worry about anything, but in everything by prayer and supplication with thanksgiving let your requests be made known to God. And the peace of God, which surpasses all understanding, will guard your hearts and your minds in Christ Jesus. (Romans 8:38-39)

Gratitude is everything in life. Gratitude connects us with the abundant resources of the universe, and opens the door to unexpected bursts of divine energy and creativity. When we are grateful, we experience a friendly universe, despite apparent scarcity and failure.

Along with "help" and "praise", "thanksgiving" is the primordial prayer. When we are thankful, we realize that we have everything we need to live abundantly, love generously, and sacrifice wisely. As contemplative activist Dag Hammarskjold, who served as General Secretary of the United Nations, affirmed:

> For all that has been – thanks!
> For all that shall be – yes!

Thanksgiving is the great "yes" to the gifts of past, present, and future. In that "yes," we find a path through life's complexities, letting go of the inessential and opening to the wonder of all being.

Prayerful Decluttering. Today, give thanks for all the blessings that come your way. In everything, look for the hand of God. Look for the angels within the challenges, and the possibilities in limitations. Say "thanks" to God for every completed task and every positive encounter.

Let your prayer be one of thanksgiving: "I thank you, God, for the wonder of my life, the wonder of this moment, and the wonder of the universe. Let me live in gratitude and amazement, praising you and serving our children. Amen."

A Simple Practice. At every turn of the road, say "thanks" for any service you receive. Take a moment to express gratitude to a mentor, teacher, friend, or colleague, whether near or far. Give thanks to God in all things.

Day Thirty-Nine
Affirmative Faith

Finally, beloved, whatever is true, whatever is honorable, whatever is just, whatever is pure, whatever is pleasing, whatever is commendable, if there is any excellence and if there is anything worthy of praise, think about [these things. Keep on doing the things that you have learned and received and heard and seen in me, and the God of peace will be with you. (Philippians 4:8-9)

Over the past six weeks, we have sought to unclutter our homes, our hearts, and our heads. Oftentimes are minds are cluttered with unnecessary and unhelpful thoughts, what Buddhist teachers call "the monkey mind." Throughout the day, we find ourselves upset by the news, other drivers on the road, and our own foolishness. Our self-talk is cluttered by a plethora of negative thoughts about ourselves and those around us. We need a healing of the mind.

The apostle says "think on these things." Our thoughts are a type of soul food, and many of us suffer from spiritual malnutrition. So, be careful of what you think about, just as should be careful about your diet and household expenses. You can practice a form of spiritual decluttering by cleansing your mind of negative and adversarial thoughts. You can also purge your mind of false limitations. In Philippians, Paul asserts, "I can do all things through Christ who strengthens me" (Philippians 4:13) and "God will fully satisfy every need of yours according to his riches in glory in Christ Jesus." (Philippians 4:19) While we may not be able to leap tall buildings at a single bound or bend steel with our bare hands, faith in God and God's power and wisdom within us opens us to new dimensions of life and greater flows of energy.

We prune the branches so the light flows through. Connected to the vine, we can do great things. Spiritual affirmations open the door to healthy thoughts and wise actions for us and those around us. Focus on positive, life-supporting, and healing thoughts as you go through the day, and you will be a blessing to your world.

Spiritual Decluttering. How cluttered is your mind with negative and limiting thinking? Throughout the day, observe your thoughts. What do they say about others and about yourself? Do you regularly practice negative self-talk? Do you accept unnecessary limits? Take time to observe and judge the accuracy of your thinking and challenge your negativity, without judgment or shame.

Let this be your prayer: "Open our minds and hearts to abundance. Deliver me from limited thinking. Deliver me from negativity. Open me to your abundant life and love. Amen.

A Simple Practice. Throughout the day, repeat the following affirmations: "I can do all things through Christ who strengthens me" and "My God will supply all my needs according to God's glory and abundance."

Day Forty
Nothing Can Separate Us From The Love Of God

> *For I am convinced that neither death, nor life, nor angels, nor rulers, nor things present, nor things to come, nor powers, nor height, nor depth, nor anything else in all creation, will be able to separate us from the love of God in Christ Jesus our Lord.* (Romans 8:38-39)

The process of spiritual decluttering is ultimately about trusting the universe, and the divine providence that guides cells, souls, and galaxies, to support your life. In the uncertainty of the world, we struggle with issues of basic trust from the very beginning. We are the imperfect children of imperfect parents, born into an imperfect social order that thwarts as well as supports our deepest desires. Often, we seek to respond to the uncertainties of life by building walls that separate us from others, hiding our feelings for fear that we will be judged, or consuming resources to fill our spiritual void. Persons of faith, whether Christian or non-Christian, trust that there is a Reality that supports our deepest desires. This Divine reality is the solid rock that sustains us when we hit rock bottom.

Trusting that God is in our side and that nothing can separate us from God's love, we can prune away everything that stands between us and God's vision for our lives. We can discard all the false gods – consumerism, security, power, and popularity – and trust a Reality that never abandons or disappoints.

We can trust that in living and dying we belong to God, and that God has never lost one of God's children, and that God will never lose us. We can live joyfully, creatively, and courageously, sacrificing for the well-being of our planet, knowing that God is with us and that nothing can separate us from the love of God.

Prayerful Decluttering. As we conclude our journey, visualize yourself in the unending circle of God's love. You are safe, strong, and secure in the care of God, whose center is everywhere, and right where you are, and whose circumference is nowhere, without beginning or end, stretching out into infinite space and time.

Let this be our prayer: "Loving God, help me to trust your circle of love, and from this place of trust, live gracefully, courageously, lovingly, and sacrificially to bring healing and love to the world. Amen."

A Simple Practice. Throughout the day, either through movement or in your imagination practice the Celtic Christian "encircling prayer." Draw a circle around yourself, rotating slowly clockwise, as you repeat an affirmation such as:

> *Circle of love.*
>
> *Open my heart.*
>
> *Circle of wisdom,*
>
> *Enlighten my thoughts*
>
> *Circle of trust,*
>
> *Protect my path.*

Circle of healing,

Grant me new life.

As you go forth on your adventures, may you experience the companionship of Christ every step of the way, and may you discover grace in your spiritual decluttering as you "turn round right."

+ + +

GROUP STUDY QUESTIONS

SESSION ONE

Introductory Chapters 1-4

Begin the session with introductions: you may share your name and, without compulsion, share why you decided to share in this spiritual journey? Where do you most need to declutter, spiritually and domestically?

After the introductions, take a few moments for silent prayer and then ask a blessing on the class, such as the following: *Loving God, we thank you for your love for us. We thank you for your presence in our lives and the chance to begin again. Help us to be attentive to your spirit of simplicity. Help us trust you as we simplify our lives, letting go of the inessential so that we can love you and your children more deeply. Amen.*

1) Looking at your life, where do you experience clutter? How does it shape your life?
2) What does abundant life mean to you? What do you need to live abundantly?
3) Read the story of Mary and Martha. (Luke 10:38-42) With whom do you most identify in the gospel story – Mary or Martha? In what ways does each of the two sisters balance and enrich the other?
4) What is your attitude toward time? Do you have "too much," "too little," or "just enough?" Do you feel like you need to prove your self-worth by being busy?
5) If you knew that you had only three months to live, how would you spend that time? Does the recognition that you are mortal change how you look at time and your priorities?

6) Do you have a sacred space? Is your home a sacred space? How could you make your home more reflective of your spiritual values?

7) How do you respond to the counsel, "live simply so others might simply live?" Do you see the connection between your lifestyle and our nation's values and the well-being of others and the environment? What are you willing to sacrifice for the well-being of our nations and the earth's most vulnerable people?

Conclude this session by lifting up one thing for which you are grateful. Then, let the leader name each member of the group and as each person's name is mentioned, let the group pray for him or her, and let each one accept a blessing for the weeks ahead. *"Loving God, bless us on our journey of spiritual decluttering. Help us be faithful to our calling as your disciples, blessing each other by your grace. Amen."*

SESSION TWO

Week One

Begin this session with a time of silent breath prayer, guided by the words: "I breathe the Spirit deeply in/And blow it gratefully out again." Follow this with a short prayer, such as: *"Loving God, open us to your abundant life so that we might bless others. Amen."*

1) When (or where) do you feel most connected with life? What gives you great joy on a regular basis? Do you take time to nurture times of joy?

2) Where do you see beauty? What did you notice when you took a "beauty walk," praying with your eyes open? How might you add beauty to your life?

3) How do you feel when you hear that you are God's beloved child, created in God's image? How might this change your life, if you really believed God's affirmation of your identity?

4) Do you regularly make time for Sabbath? How might you integrate a flexible Sabbath into your life?

5) In what ways might you deepen your relationships with loved ones or embark on new relationships?

6) Do you have a contemplative practice? What prayerful practices have been most helpful to you? What spiritual practices would nurture your spirit at this time?

7) What one area of your weekly schedule can you declutter to deepen your relationship with God and your significant others? What would you have to give up to experience less spiritual clutter in your life?

Conclude with a blessing for each group member, and the prayer: *"Help me, O God, to recognize that I am loved just as I am. Let me accept your graceful blessing so that I might bless others. Amen."*

Session Three

Week Two

Begin with a moment of silence. Then share an insight you experienced in the previous week, followed by an opening prayer, such as *"God of new beginnings, your mercies are new every morning. Help me experience your transforming love and dare to explore new behaviors and ways of looking at the world. Amen."*

1) Where do you need to leave the familiar to experience God's vision of simplicity in your life? What are the risks of change? What are the gifts of change?

2) What was it like to attempt the practice of "blessing" everyone you meet? How did it change your perception of others and yourself?

3) Do you have a personal altar? How does it change your life to have a particular ritual or place to center your spirit?

4) Where have you found gateways to heaven in your life? Have you ever found insight or guidance through dreams?

5) What issues of faith are most challenging for you? What issues keep you up at night, looking for answers or seeking peace amid conflict?

6) Looking at your "home economics," do you set aside financial resources for the future? What is the greatest challenge for your stewardship of your personal resources? Where do you need to "save" and where do you need to "give away" in your stewardship?

7) How does the phenomenon of "busyness" shape your life? How do you feel when you are "busy?" Do you have antidotes to feeling busy or stressed?

Conclude with a time of blessing for each group member, followed by practicing the Celtic prayer of encircling. Either standing or sitting draw a circle around yourself as you pray: "*Encircle me with love, encircle me with peace, encircle me with joy. Amen.*"

SESSION FOUR

Week Three

Begin with a time of silence, and then recite the Lord's Prayer. Take a moment for time to share "God moments" that were experienced during the week. Let the prayer of the day be: *"We give thanks for beauty, wonder, and love. Open our senses to your wisdom, Loving Creator, and give us grace to share our gifts with others. Amen."*

1. What are the biggest challenges in your experiencing of peace in your life? What stands in the way of you becoming a peacemaker in your world?
2. Do you have a personal vision statement that guides your life? Take a moment and craft an affirmation that can serve as a personal vision, guiding you in your decisions throughout the day and over the long haul.
3. How would you respond if the Living God encountered you in the church sanctuary, as God did Isaiah in the Temple? Do you believe God has a purpose for your life? What purposes or vocations inspire you these days?
4. Reflecting on Micah 6:8, consider the following questions: What does it mean for you to practice kindness in a time of political polarization and national division? What is the meaning of justice in a society whose decisions often favor the wealthy over the poor and the powerful over the dispossessed? In what ways can your life give witness to Gods' vision of Shalom and justice for all creation?
5. As we continue to consider how we can be agents of justice, consider the following questions: Where is your lifestyle complicit in social and economic behaviors? Where are you benefited indirectly by the pain of others? Are there ways you can live more justly personally and in your citizenship?

6. Often people feel powerless to effect any change in the world. Looking at your life, in what one area can you make a difference to people around you and to the society in which you live?

7. In the past week, you were asked to pray for issues in the daily news. What issues touched your heart? What issues called you to prayer? Were you inspired to any actions in response?

8. Read Micah 8, followed by sharing areas of pain in the world as a call to intercession. Lift up prayerfully each issue and ask for God's guidance. *"God of Justice and Peace, open our senses to the pain of the world. Guide us so that we might respond with compassion and care as your companions in healing the world. Amen."*

SESSION FIVE

Week Four

Begin with a time of stillness, awakening to God's presence in the group. Meditatively read Matthew 5:14-16, awakening to the light within you and the group. Take a few moments in silence to breathe deeply the light of God, letting it fill you and then imagine a circle of light connecting the group. Let this be your prayer: *"Light of the World shine in me, on me, through me. Let there be light in this place and let us be beacons of light bringing light to our world. Amen."*

1) Where do you see yourself most blessed? What is your criteria for defining a blessing? Have you ever been blessed by experiences or situations that, at first glance, appeared negative or unwanted?

2) Where do you see God's light in yourself? Where do you see God's light in others? Were you able to bring God's light to any particular situations this week?

3) Did you experience anger this week? How did you respond to feelings of anger? Do you feel your anger or response was justified? In what ways can anger clutter our lives? In what ways can anger be a catalyst for change and healing?

4) Do you have any "enemies?" Do you have any persons for whom you have no respect and interpret as malevolent? In what ways do you respond to these persons? In what ways can you heal your relationship with your enemies?

5) What would it mean for you to live out the counsel, "thy kingdom come, thy will be done, on earth as it is in heaven?" What first steps can you take to make earth a heavenly place?

6) On day five, you were asked about what you would retrieve if your house was on fire. What things came to mind? What does that say about your priorities? Looking at your life, what

is your treasure? Are you pleased with this "treasure?" If not, what do you need to do to find a true treasure? What physical, relational, or spiritual things do you need to jettison to find your true treasure?

7) Looking at your life, what do you perceive to be your greatest need? Do you trust God to respond to your deepest need? How would seeking God's realm first and above all else change your attitude toward life and its challenges? What do you need to declutter to trust God more fully?

Conclude your time by lifting up one person who is in need of God's love (you don't need to mention their name, if confidentiality is important in the situation). As you go around the circle, lift up one area where you feel a need for grace or healing and one area where you need to declutter. Go around the circle, naming each person, and then affirming, "God will provide for your deepest needs." Let this be your prayer: *"God of sparrows and lilies, whales and hummingbirds, help us trust you with our deepest needs and with our response to those in need. Give us wisdom, courage, and compassion. Amen."*

SESSION SIX

Week Five

After a time of silence, meditatively read Matthew 6:25-30, 32b-34). Share any insights from the scripture, followed by the prayer: *"Loving Parent, who clothes the lilies and feeds the birds, help us to trust your resources and in trusting, share with others, blessed to be a blessing for all we meet. Amen."*

1. What do you judge in others? What do you judge about yourself? What self-talk do you use for yourself and others? How does this self-talk shape your attitudes toward self and others? Are your judgements warranted or helpful in your quest for wholeness?

2. Do you ever pray for certain outcomes for yourself or others? Have you ever made bold requests of God? Did you receive a response? Was it what you expected?

3. If God is best known by subtraction, what do you need to subtract to experience God knocking at the door of your life? Are you willing to subtract to have a deeper relationship with God?

4. Upon what rock do you build your life? What do you trust when the going gets tough? Is the object of your trust reliable in times of stress and storm?

5. What are your five loaves and two fish? What are your perceived resources in time, talent, and treasure? How do you feel about your resources? Do you feel limited or abundant? In what ways might you multiply your resources for God's glory and the well-being of those around you?

6. Do you currently have any storms in your life? How would your perception of these storms change if you knew that Jesus was in the boat with you?

7. As you look at your life, what takes your eyes off Jesus? What helps you stay focused on Jesus' or God's presence in your life? What do you need to declutter to have greater focus on God's saving presence in your life?

Conclude with each person reflecting on their "five loaves and two fish" and the promise of God's abundance within our perceived scarcity. Let us pray: *"Bless my resources that I might bless others. Multiply my gifts and talents, my resources, so that I can share generously with those around me?*

SESSION SEVEN

Week Six

Begin your time together with each person sharing one blessing for which he or she is particularly grateful. Let us pray: *"Give me a grateful heart and a spirit of service that I might by God's grace and guidance bring healing and love to my world. Amen."*

1) Looking at your relationship to our cultural values, what are your greatest temptations in relationship to our culture? Where are you most likely to "conform" to the world? In what ways might you experience the transformation grounded in an alternative set of values?

2) As you look at your life, can you identify a "good work" God is doing? How can you nurture God's good work? What do you need to prune away for God's harvest to flourish in your life?

3) The apostle Paul counsels, "Do not worry about anything, but in everything by prayer and supplication with thanksgiving let your requests be made known to God." What are your primary worries? In what ways is gratitude an antidote for worry?

4) What do you say when you talk to yourself? What is the quality of your self-talk? What words of affirmation do you need to hear? What words do you need to say to yourself?

5) What threatens to separate you from God or defeat your personal hopes and dreams? In what ways does Paul's affirmation "nothing can separate us from the love of God," transform our lives?

As we conclude our study, for what are you most thankful in our time together? Where have you grown? What clutter was most necessary to give up? What clutter was most difficult to give up?

Around the circle, naming each member one by one, let each other member share one affirmation about him or her. Close the study with the Celtic encircling and the prayer on the fortieth day:

> *Circle of love.*
>
> *Open my heart.*
>
> *Circle of wisdom,*
>
> *Enlighten my thoughts.*
>
> *Circle of trust,*
>
> *Protect my path.*
>
> *Circle of healing,*
>
> *Grant me new life.*

www.ingramcontent.com/pod-product-compliance
Lightning Source LLC
LaVergne TN
LVHW041229080426
835508LV00011B/1129